BECAUSE I HAVE TO

Cover photograph: *After Night (cotton field), 2011*, by Lisa Ross.
Cover and book design: Alex Dimeff.

Library of Congress Cataloging-in-Publication Data

Names: Ilham, Jewher, author.
Title: Because I have to : the path to survival, the Uyghur struggle / by
  Jewher Ilham.
Other titles: Path to survival, the Uyghur struggle
Description: New Orleans, Louisiana : University of New Orleans Press,
  [2021]
Identifiers: LCCN 2021031997 | ISBN 9781608012275 (paperback) | ISBN
  9781608012329 (ebook)
Subjects: LCSH: Ilham, Jewher. | Uighur (Turkic
  people)--China--Beijing--Biography. | Political
  activists--China--Biography. | College
  students--Indiana--Bloomington--Biography. | Uighur (Turkic
  people)--Ethnic identity. | Uighur (Turkic people)--Civil rights--China.
  | Ilham, Jewher--Family. | Political refugees--United States--Biography.
Classification: LCC DS731.U4 I53 2021 | DDC 362.82/95092 [B]--dc23
LC record available at https://lccn.loc.gov/2021031997

Printed in the United States of America on acid-free paper.

UNIVERSITY OF NEW ORLEANS PRESS
2000 Lakeshore Drive
New Orleans, Louisiana 70148
unopress.org

BECAUSE I HAVE TO

the path to survival, the uyghur struggle

by JEWHER ILHAM

series editor: Adam Braver

foreword by Sophie Richardson
afterword by Clare Robinson

includes interviews with Tahir Hamut,
Mihrigul Tursun, and Akida Paluti

UNIVERSITY OF NEW ORLEANS PRESS

About the Cover Art
Lisa Ross, photographer

After Night is a series of photographs I made over a number of years (2002-2011) in the Turpan Prefecture of the Uyghur Region. During the day, beds are placed outdoors to await nightfall, until their owners come to sleep on them under the night sky, escaping the heat trapped indoors from the summer's sun. In Turpan, there has been a long tradition of placing beds on rooftops, in front of homes, in fields near grape drying houses and vineyards.

A magical dreamscape and poetic perceptions of freedom inspired the vision of this work. Now, as I go through my archive of images from the Uyghur Region, all is reconsidered, revisited and re-evaluated in the context of the Chinese government's efforts to erase Uyghur culture, identity and the very people who have created, maintained and valued it.

For example, in 2019 we have learned that cotton production is one of the greatest exports utilizing forced labor in the Xinjiang region, affecting the reading of the photograph on this cover titled, *After Night (cotton field), 2011.*

The images have all taken on a very different meaning.

For more about Lisa Ross and her work, visit: StudioLisaRoss.com

Foreword

Sophie Richardson,
China Director, Human Rights Watch

One could say that this book reflects Jewher Ilham, whom I first met in April 2014, and who published the first part of her story the following November, simply getting older. Her steely spine, profound kindness, and conviction were already visible then—despite the trauma of being separated from her family, having to navigate English and the United States and university, and to make tough decisions about how to proceed in this unimaginable phase of life.

Her first book concluded with a reply to an interviewer's question, asking whether she wanted to add any other thoughts: "No, I think that is everything. For now."

But that "now" feels like a lifetime ago, and this new book reflects that at personal, community, and global levels. It also shows the very human toll on Jewher, and her considered embrace of activism on behalf not only of her father but also her community.

Right about the same time as that "now" in 2014, Chinese authorities launched a "Strike Hard Against Violent Extremism" campaign across Xinjiang. The repression of Uyghurs and other Turkic communities is longstanding, but it has accelerated significantly, and is vast: mass detention facilities, Orwellian high-tech surveillance, Chinese Communist Party cadres sleeping in families' beds, cultural devastation—bulldozing mosques, paving over Muslim cemeteries, erasing Uyghur language—on an unprecedented scale.

Jewher's new book shows how acutely aware she is of the state's hostility towards her community and family, not least through the baseless prosecution of her father, Uyghur economist Ilham Tohti, who in 2014 was sentenced to life in prison. She also likens Beijing's policies to "boiling frogs," and laments that all of her Uyghur friends have been forced off social media. But does she feel sorry for herself? No. She sees that deafening silence as a critical development to mobilizing global concern about Xinjiang: "Honestly, I would rather feel alone again because that would mean nobody would have to suffer what I've suffered." Her sense of commitment to her community is also on display: interspersed between chapters telling her own story she gives the stage to other Uyghurs, including Tahir Hamut and Mihrigul Tursun, who themselves survived human rights abuses at the hands of Chinese authorities.

Perhaps the toughest part of recent years for Jewher personally and the broader academic-activist community: the sudden death in January 2017 of Elliot Sperling, a well-known scholar of Sino-Tibetan relations. A longtime friend of Jewher's father, it was Sperling who received Jewher in the US following her father's arrest at the Beijing airport, and who effectively adopted and guided her through university, graduation, and into her activist phase. She credits him not only with serving as a father figure but also with teaching her "how to fight for every good person."

The book unfolds over what has been one of the most contentious periods of any modern Chinese leadership's relationship with the United States, other governments, and international institutions. While Xi Jinping wasted no time consolidating power after assuming the top position in 2013, global opinion has hardened as evidence of harsh abuses in Xinjiang and Hong Kong dominated headlines, as Chinese government-backed Belt and Road Initiative projects go awry, and especially as Beijing has remained intransigent about the origins of the coronavirus pandemic. Some governments, parliaments, and institutions like the United Nations Human Rights Council now recognize that they too might be frogs to be boiled by Beijing.

Jewher speaks to this change by chronicling high-profile meetings and receiving awards on her father's behalf, a journey that takes her from Donald Trump's Oval Office to the European Parliament. But this is all layered on top of her reflections about her growing Uyghur pride: cooking traditional foods, dancing traditional dances, mulling her faith, even working on her Uyghur language skills.

This book is a remarkable window into Jewher's transformation from having harbored "teenager hopes" through to her decision to pursue independent activism, and all while paying an enormous personal cost. She is cut off from most of her family, deprived of her real and adoptive fathers, and walking a political highwire. But she does so with grace, humor, and insight. One only hopes a third book is not necessary.

July 19, 2021

Editor's Note

Adam Braver,
Broken Silence Series Editor

For those coming to Jewher Ilham's story for the first time and may be unfamiliar with it, it is important to understand that her story is one of her father's plight. Ilham Tohti was born in Artush, in the Uyghur region. He moved to Beijing as graduate student to study economics, where he eventually settled into an associate professorship at Minzu University. In 2006 he founded a website called *Uyghur Online*. While the site was often critical of Chinese policy toward the Uyghur people in the so-called Xinjiang region, the intent always focused on forging solutions for a peaceful and respectful coexistence. It is in this context that Ilham became known as a "moderate voice."

Soon Ilham caught the attention of the Chinese authorities—this moderate voice now became portrayed as someone who was inciting violence, and even worse, advocating separatism. Several times he was detained. Placed under house arrest. Threatened. And yet he persevered with his work on *Uyghur Online*, still envisioning a country in which Han Chinese and Uyghur people could co-exist beyond the inherent and historical tensions.

In 2013, he agreed to come to Indiana University for one year as a visiting scholar. He planned to bring his eighteen-year-old, Beijing-born daughter, Jewher, with him. She would stay for just one month during her winter school break. But as they prepared to board the plane, Ilham suddenly was detained, and in the mayhem, Jewher ended up alone on the U.S. bound flight, after her father, while in police custody at the airport, implored her to go to the U.S. and to never come back.

One year later, after a continuing pattern of threats and house arrests, Ilham was arrested and detained, and almost eight months later was formally charged for "separatism"—a charge that could bring the death penalty at its worst, and a life sentence at its best.

The prospect for Jewher ever being able to return safely to China had diminished.

In 2014 Ilham Tohti was tried on manufactured charges of "separatism." Highlighting China's repression of Uyghurs (and of its general aggressive attitude toward human rights), the case caught the attention of the global media and of world leaders. It became the main avenue for introducing the plight of Uyghurs in China (something that unfortunately would only grow and grow in the coming years). Already there were many questions being raised about the fairness of the trial. For example, why was it being held in the high-tension Uyghur region when the alleged crime was committed nearly 1,500 miles away in Beijing (not to mention where he had his *hukou*—his registered permanent residency)? Why was Ilham's lawyer denied access to certain pieces of evidence? Were the proceedings really being closed because of state secrets? To many international observers, there was a sense that this only would be a show trial. That the Chinese Authority's belief already had been cemented that Ilham Tohti had, as the *New York Times* reported, "'bewitched and coerced young ethnic students' into working on his website and that he had 'built a criminal syndicate' . . . and 'internationalized' the Uighur issue by giving interviews to foreign reporters and had translated foreign articles and essays about Xinjiang to be posted on *Uighur Online*."

It is at that point, after the guilty verdict was returned and Ilham now awaited his sentence, where Jewher's first book, *Jewher Ilham: A Uyghur's Fight to Free Her Father*, left off.

For those coming to *Because I Have To* already with an understanding of the situation, or perhaps as a companion to the previous book, I would encourage those readers to consider the changing world that took place between the past and present of

Jewher's story, namely the mass internment and diaspora perpetrated on the Uyghur people by the Chinese government. And equally important is the blossoming that happened within its author, one that now reveals an even higher level of dignity and grace in facing what, simply put, is an awful story, one that we, as a world, should be ashamed to be telling, and yet one that should leave us inspired by the passion and dedication of Jewher, who in the tradition of her father works to navigate this crisis toward a peaceful and positive outcome.

Many thanks to the people at UNO Press for their professionalism, and for their support (and sometimes bravery) for being willing to bring stories such as this one into the public consciousness. Equally important are my friends and colleagues on Scholars at Risk's Advocacy Team, as well as the volumes of global faculty and students who I have come to admire as we've worked together on behalf on Ilham Tohti and other unfairly detained scholars worldwide. Also, thanks to Kieran Binney, who helped with early shaping of the transcripts for this book, and to the support of colleagues at the Roger Williams University Library. And lastly, of course, I can't forget Jewher, who, through nearly eight years of friendship, has inspired me, and pushed me, to be a better and kinder person.

PART ONE

A Little Piece of Memory
in My Heart

The Sentencing

In China it was Wednesday morning. But in Bloomington it was still Tuesday night. September 23, 2014. My roommate and I were on the floor. We didn't care where we sat. We just wanted to find a spot and stay there.

The news would be coming at any minute.

All I was doing was staring at my phone, refreshing the page. Over and over. Waiting for news of the sentencing.

It was just like when my dad first had been taken away just after I'd arrived in the US. Then, I'd been refreshing the page to find out if he'd actually been arrested, or, if just like every other time the authorities would detain, threaten, and harass him, and then he'd be sent back home. But now, less than a year later, here we were—the same bad thing, just a different day.

I froze when I finally got the news. I turned to my roommate, and said, "*Wúqī...*无期"—Chinese for *life sentence.*

I started to cry. And when I stopped, I just cried again. I could barely process the information. My brain was a mess. Like a ball of yarn that a cat has played with, all messed up.

Journalists started calling, wanting my first-time reaction. I understood it; they needed to write their articles. But I just let the phone ring. I had no idea how to react. At least seven or eight reporters phoned within a few minutes.

Finally I picked up one call. (I don't even remember from which news agency.) They asked if I'd read about the news, *da da da da.* "What's your reaction about it?"

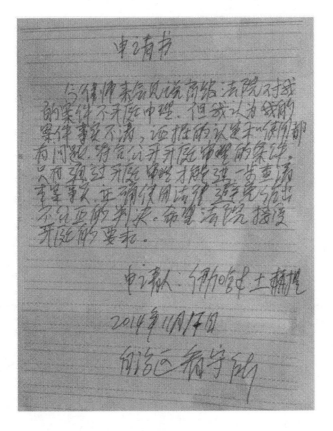

An application my father wrote from prison, disputing the closed-door
proceedings of his trial.

"Sorry," I said. "I don't want to comment on anything. I hope
you understand." I hung up as quick as I could.

And then a text message came from another journalist, basically asking the same question. I shot back a reply, saying, "Sorry.
I don't want to say anything. Hope you understand."

"Would you mind speaking to me tomorrow then?"

All I could think was, *What are you even talking about? My dad
just got sentenced to life in prison. And you're only thinking about
getting my first-time reaction?*

What did I do next? Did I say something to my roommate? Did I call Elliot[1]?

I can't remember.

Except for those immediate moments when I first heard the news, it's all very blurry. I'm sure Elliot encouraged me a lot, but I just can't think of it very clearly.

It's like how some people, when they are so traumatized, choose to forget. I think maybe that was it.

During my father's trial.

I was expecting five years. Elliot thought it could be as much as ten, if the Chinese government really wanted to make a point. No one imagined it could be a life sentence.

---

1   Elliot Sperling, a professor of Central Eurasian Studies at Indiana University, had been Jewher's protector, advocate, and confidant after she arrived unexpectedly alone in the US in February 2013, following her father's detainment at the airport in Beijing, and his subsequent arrest and detainment.

There's a short video clip of my dad walking really confidently into the courtroom in Ürümqi, knowing that he did not do anything wrong. Even after he was sentenced to life, he said, "I don't accept this." He was pointing with one finger. That was something he always did when he wanted to make a point.

My dad was the first political prisoner in China to receive a life sentence since the Cultural Revolution. *The first*. Not only among Uyghurs but also among Han Chinese.

At the trial and in the prison, he was shackled—with not only restraints around his hands but also heavy chains on his feet. He never killed anybody or harmed anyone. Why would he need to be shackled like that?

He's a scholar. He doesn't even work out or lift weights. The only thing he ever uses is his pen; that's the heaviest exercise equipment he has.

The day after the trial, my stepmom and my uncles were able to visit my father with his lawyer. Inside the prison, my dad told the lawyer, "To be honest, after nine months, last night was the first time I was able to sleep well."

The lawyer asked, "Why? What do you mean?"

"I thought I was going to be given the death penalty. A life sentence is not too bad. It's fine."

I almost teared up when I heard this because in my imagination that's how my father would respond. I had imagined him saying similar things because he's so positive, with hope for everything.

Activism and Asylum

Up until the trial, I really believed that my father was going to get out, that I'd be able to see him again. The verdict was like a big slap in the face.

For a while, I was even questioning myself. Did I make this happen to him? Did my advocacy work actually make it worse?

I remember I had this conversation with Elliot, not long after the trial. I said, "What if it's because of me?"

"No. It's never because of you," he said. "You're not the oppressor. The government is. The government arrested him. You did not do anything illegal. Your dad did not do anything illegal. You can never blame yourself because you are doing the right thing. Even if the government claims this sentence is because of your advocacy work, it's their minds that are twisted. It's not because of your actions."

And now I use this theory to comfort other people, especially young advocates who contact me because they have relatives in prison. They tell me they wish they had the courage to do what I have been doing on behalf of my dad. But they say, "I am afraid that if the government does something more, then it will be my fault."

I begin, "Once somebody told me this . . ." And I say the exact same thing Elliot told me.

This is the real truth: I did not arrest over one million people. I did not put Uyghur people in concentration camps or in labor camps. I did not torture them. I did not do anything for my own benefit. None of us who are so-called "victims" did. The government is doing that. They try to make it seem as if it's your own fault. Like an abuser who says, "If you didn't make me so mad,

I wouldn't have had to hit you," they try to make people feel responsible for what happens to them because the abuser actually knows his actions are bad. They always need to find the scapegoat.

Many of us have friends and relatives who were told by the police that the problems for Uyghurs come from other Uyghurs overseas. The government even works to create distrust among some parts of the Uyghur community. Their reversal strategy is meant to mess with our minds so that we'll silence ourselves. As if we're doing it by choice. In the end, their hope is that we'll be as voiceless as the other Uyghurs in China.

This is a common tactic among authoritarian governments—they blame all of their outrageous atrocities on the citizens.

As Elliot reminded me so many times: "Even if you shut up, they're still going to do what they are doing to your father."

Before my dad was sentenced, I was going pretty mild with my advocacy work. I didn't seek out opportunities to speak up; I only appeared at those that were given to me. But after the sentencing, I started to go into attack mode. Marching forward instead of waiting to be asked to do something.

Before the sentencing, I was still hoping that the authorities were going to release my dad (just as they did after every other arrest). I thought: *I'll be going back to China. I'll be going back to the college that I was in. I'll be going to live with my parents again happily and forever, end of story.* I was still having teenager hopes, where everything was like a fairy tale, and all I'd been through was just another type of adventure.

But after my father was sentenced, I understood that the possibility of ever going back to China safely had become so much smaller. Almost invisible.

It may sound naive, but even today, I maintain hope.

The Good and Bad in Everything

My dad knew that he was going to go to prison. He knew his family was being affected by his work on behalf of Uyghurs.

So why would he continue?

Because, as he would say, it is the right thing to do.

Chinese people accuse me of bringing shame on China by showing its ugly side. And some Uyghur people have even accused me of being too moderate. I get accused of many different things.

But that's okay. My only intention is to speak the truth.

I will support what I think is right. If my dad were actually a separatist, an extremist, and someone who supported violence, it's very unlikely that I would work this hard to get him out of prison. Like my dad, I care most about what I think is the "right thing."

I try really hard not to hate China. I spent eighteen years there—my entire childhood. It's the place where some of the most important events of my life happened. It's a little piece of memory in my heart.

I try not to ignore that there are some good sides of China and only target the bad side. I need to be honest about it—even when it comes to what the Chinese leadership has been doing to the Uyghurs over the past year, something so horrific, something so evil, an atrocity I've dedicated my life to fighting. But that's the difference between the Chinese government and me; they will only see the bad in my father or me—and in my people.

My dad thought the same way: he was willing to acknowledge the good and bad in everything.

Why would he have ignored the good parts, especially when his goal was to create dialogue between Han and Uyghurs? He understood that a meaningful dialogue is based on the ability to see and acknowledge the positive and negative on both sides. But as we saw, despite my dad's best efforts, the Chinese government only could focus on his criticisms about the government. They ignored my dad when he would acknowledge them for making certain positive decisions and policies. He'd publicly say things like "That's pretty good. Keep with it. Don't lose that good thing." But people see what they want to see.

I apply this philosophy to my daily life, not just to advocacy. The good should be called out. The bad should be called out. But you can still respect the person or the institution. Isn't that how you get to a place of understanding and mutual respect?

Culturally Muslim

My religion was a source of support during my dad's sentencing. When Ramadan came in summer 2014, I didn't know what would happen with the trial, but I did know that bad things were happening to my dad since his arrest. And so I fasted every single day, keeping up with everything. By choosing to be more faithful, I wasn't so much thinking about getting my dad released. Instead I was hoping that Allah would answer my prayers, and bring some ease to my father's situation.

Islam plays a huge part in Uyghur culture. But for me, having grown up in Beijing, I hadn't lived in that culture. The concept of being a Muslim was very vague. I knew I was Uyghur. I knew I was Muslim. I knew I couldn't eat pork. I knew I couldn't drink alcohol. But other than people telling me that, I didn't really know why.

But after coming here to the US and learning more about Islam and having so many Muslim friends, for the first time I came to understand why my grandma did this, why my uncle did that, why my aunt did this, why my stepmom did that. Everything now made sense.

Oddly, here I have the freedom to engage in my Islamic heritage. Nobody limits you. For example, there was a mosque just fifteen minutes away from one of my classrooms in Bloomington. What would be the odds of that in Beijing? And anyone could just go to that mosque without an appointment. During Ramadan there are so many families that cook huge amounts of food and bring it to the mosque just so everyone can have it. They don't deny non-Muslims entry to get food.

I found it so fascinating because I never got to see this side of Islam in Beijing.

After all these years, I still wouldn't consider myself a "good" Muslim; instead, I'd consider myself as a Muslim who is still learning. It's a lifelong path.

Being Uyghur Outside China

Ironically, even though I'm so distant from my homeland, living in another country, I actually have more connection to Uyghur culture, Uyghur identity, and Uyghur heritage than ever.

In Beijing I could count on both hands the Uyghurs I knew outside of my family—mostly my family's coworkers, some distant friends, or some of my father's students. But now I see that learning about each other—and talking more to each other about our heritage—is how we try to reduce the physical distance between one another.

In fact, I took a Uyghur class at IU, which was extremely helpful. Can you imagine? I learned my own mother tongue in another country! Now I know how to read. I know how to write. I can even understand advanced level Uyghur news articles and radio programs. As a child, I never imagined I would be able to do that. I can't wait to speak or write to my father in Uyghur. One day.

A Family Trip

The year before I came to the US, we all went on a twenty-day road trip—my dad, my stepmom, my brother . . . and a few policemen. We traveled through half of the Uyghur region, also known among the Chinese as Xinjiang. Ürümqi, Hotan, Kanas Lake at Altay, and Sayram Lake in Bortala—all the famous tourist spots. I remember before we went, I was strongly against it. Against that idea when my dad said, "Let's do a road trip to Xinjiang."

"No!" said. "I want to stay in Beijing! No!" It was the summer of my second year of high school.

"Ah, next year you will be studying for for *gāokǎo*.[2] You won't have the chance to go with me to Xinjiang for the next couple of years. This will be your last chance."

And indeed it became our last chance. It was the first and only time that I actually really traveled with my dad back to my hometown. We'd been to the Uyghur region together in the past, but only for family visits, not as tourists who were traveling, site-seeing, and learning.

The three police officers rode with us in a small bus with nine seats. One lady, two guys. I never thought of them as *police*-police. I thought their job just happened to be with the police department, and that somehow they were just our family acquaintances.

I was so young and naïve.

They appeared pretty friendly with my dad. I already knew one of the police officers. It turns out he was assigned to monitor my dad because he was Hui;[3] the State Security thought my dad

---

2   The Chinese SAT
3   The majority of the Hui people are Chinese-speaking practioners of Islam.

would let his guard down around him. I always thought he was my father's friend.

He spent a lot of time with my family. He would drink tea with us. Eat with us. Sometimes sleep over at our apartment. Even though he was following his obligations and duties, I also can't believe that after all that time he didn't get attached to us. I'm sure he felt really sad when he saw what happened to my dad. I remember him saying to my father once, "You're such a great person. I wish we didn't meet under these circumstances, and then we could be real friends." And, yes, even though he may have been part of what caused it to happen, it's not his fault. It's the system.

I hope he can hear this. I hope he knows that I don't blame him.

A family trip to the Uyghur Region, Summer 2011.

Luck

I am lucky and unlucky at the same time.

I'm unlucky in that bad things happen to my family and to me, but I am lucky because I always have someone—strangers or acquaintances or friends or families—who seems to appear and be there for me when I need them the most. Sometimes they don't even know how helpful they're being. Since I've been in the US, I've always had someone help me go through all my obstacles.

That's one of the many reasons that made Elliot's death so hard on me—suddenly the person who'd helped me get through everything was gone. Elliot had always been there for me—for *everything*. Even for things like cooking a dish. I'd call him to complain, "Elliot! I burnt this meat!"

He was always there for even small things. He could be my girly-girlfriend. He could be a serious uncle. He could be a professor and help me crack down my homework. He had so many roles that he could play: the family role, the friend role, the mentor role. That's why when he passed away, it was . . .

It was probably one of the hardest things.

PART TWO
Deep Down

After the Sentencing

After my dad got sentenced, I remember Elliot telling me that while my dad may be sentenced for life, this was not the end. Elliot said, "We have to fight even harder now."

But I wasn't sure about my actual goal. I had all kinds of contradictory feelings. Did I want to push for the Chinese government to immediately release him, which was almost impossible, since they'd sentenced him to life? Or did I want to advocate for them to shorten the sentence, which wouldn't really satisfy me because a man like my father shouldn't have been staying in jail for even one more day? I didn't know which was the more practical goal.

There is a saying: when the fly doesn't know where to go, it just keeps shaking its wings. I was like that. I would keep moving, moving, doing activities. But I didn't know where I was going or what I actually expected to come out of this.

I just knew that I needed to fight.

Attention

I was worried that people would slowly forget about my dad after he went to jail. To make sure that didn't happen, I constantly accepted interviews. They may be talking about it today, I figured, but in a week, in a month, the attention could die down.

I understood how easily the passion of "We need to get Ilham Tohti out!" could turn into "There are also other scholars. We need to work on their cases too."

So I worked to keep the news fresh. To get updates about my dad from my family in the Uyghur region, to search out details from journalists who covered the region. Anything to have new information with which to update people. Then they wouldn't forget or just say, "Oh, there's nothing new . . . Still the same case."

Even today, I guess I still worry about the same thing. I still work like a machine to prevent Ilham Tohti's name from fading away. I don't ever want him to be forgotten. I just haven't figured out what's the best way. With so little news about him coming from China, I don't know if there is a best way, to be honest.

Taking Care of Myself

I had to focus on school. I was not yet at Indiana University at that time; I was still trying to learn English at the community college. Because of what happened to my dad, my school performance kind of went down.

It was very hard to keep up fully with my schoolwork and travel all the time, skipping my exams to do advocacy work. I was afraid that if I focused on my school, then that would mean I was doing less work for my father, and therefore people's attention would die down. And yet if I focused on that advocacy work, then I'd risk failing my classes.

Elliot just told me that I needed to study harder. And he was always there to help me with my schoolwork. Regularly we would have long, long video calls just to discuss a paper. A call could go on for one to two hours. Sometimes during those discussions, we'd start talking about my dad and my dad's advocacy work. And then we'd shift back to schoolwork: the mistakes, the grammar. But then somehow it would slowly turn back to something my dad said, and then we'd find ourselves talking about him again. It just went back and forth, back and forth.

And all in English. Elliot preferred me to use it, so I could learn the language faster. It definitely helped. But I think I also improved more quickly than normal because of the advocacy work I was doing. Talking with American journalists, government people, lawyers, and NGOs. Not to mention needing to read so many articles about my dad in English. (For years, the first thing I'd do in the morning was to check news sources for information about my father.)

I knew I needed to improve my English in order to say the things I wanted to say about my dad's work and his situation. I learned the hard way! During a TV interview in 2014, after the host asked me a question, I said that I was sorry, that I didn't understand. Later that night, I told myself that I really needed to study harder because it was so embarrassing! Some people commented that it seemed like I didn't know what I was talking about. That got in my head, causing me to worry that I would bring shame to my father.

I guess that just as the good always comes along with the bad, the bad also comes along with the good. So, indeed, it's bad that I had to focus on this advocacy casework while I was trying to focus on school. But at the same time, it helped me with my schoolwork, at least with my English skills. And as my English improved, some people got suspicious about the level at which I could speak, even bringing accusations of me being trained by the CIA. I should be so flattered.

Academic Plans

My hope was to get into IU. But I knew the only chance for both a scholarship and admittance depended on my English being good enough. I had to improve it to get a better TOEFL score, in order to pass the English placement test.

My initial plan was to study journalism. The more interviews I took, the more I thought that becoming a journalist was the best way to help my dad. I thought if the day comes when nobody will interview me, then I'll write the articles and tell the world myself.

Okay, I was too young, too naïve.

I realized that because English was my weakness, journalism was going to be a very difficult path. I'd have to completely focus on English literature and writing skills to be able to get into a pretty good news agency—a news agency that was powerful enough that I could actually help my dad. Working it out, I thought I'd need at least five years to improve my English skills to the level needed to become a good journalist. I questioned if it was the most efficient path. *It's going to take me I-don't-know-how-many years*, I thought. *But I can't wait. It will be too late for him by then.*

I considered law school. But in the US, becoming a lawyer takes years and years. So I was like, "Okay, pass." What other academic career could help me to help my father?

What was another way? A faster way? I was impatient.

It was one of those first trips to Washington, DC, that got me thinking, following meetings with congresspeople, people from the State Department, and other officials. A really important moment came in 2014 when I testified at the Congressional Executive Committee on China. One of the senators asked me a question about how the situation in the Uyghur Region would affect the US-China economy. I must have looked like a rock or something. "I'm just a teenager," I wanted to say. "I don't know. I don't know how to answer this."

That moment planted the first thought that maybe I should study international relations or political science. Because studying those theories and issues would help me understand the larger context of what was happening in China and how it affected the world. At the time of that hearing, all I could really say was, "My dad, my dad, my dad." Other than that, I did not know how to answer any of the larger questions.

Once I finally got to Indiana University, I took some international relations classes and political science classes, along with Arabic classes, and a little bit of this and that. Those political science classes were hard and often quite boring. But the knowledge I learned from those classes turned out to be really, really helpful.

Muslim Ban

In 2016, Donald Trump was elected. For me, it was the first time I'd witnessed democracy in action—from debates in my classes, to seeing people able to vote for their representatives and president. I was envious. But for Elliot, he thought the outcome of the election was terrible. And based on some of Trump's campaign promises—especially the way he talked about Muslims in America, Elliot was very worried about what might happen to me if I didn't have a country to go back to safely. Every day the news was something about the Muslim bans, building the wall, and refugee deportations. It wasn't just Elliot. I was also worried. How would I carry on advocating for my dad if I had to leave?

Elliot was so concerned for me. And it made him so stressed. He was constantly in anger mode because of Trump. Outraged by Trump's actions and words.

I'd visited Elliot few weeks before he passed away, when I was in New York for a two-day UN meeting. He was so frustrated about everything, complaining that he felt like he'd aged.

For a while, I actually blamed Elliot's passing on Trump because I remembered that when Elliot got mad, his face turned so red, like his blood pressure was going up. The day when Elliot passed away was during the announcement of the Muslim ban. And I thought maybe in his anger, his heart just couldn't take it. But I don't know. We'll never know the real reason behind it.

Money

Financially, I was taken care of since I was little. Although my dad was well-off when I was a teenager, that was not the case when I was younger. Our entire apartment, a studio, would fit into my current bedroom. Whenever my grandmother visited us in Beijing, three of us would be squeezed on the bed like sardines, while my dad would sleep on the floor. But by the time I was in middle school, in addition to his teaching, my dad started getting involved in running a factory in Kazakhstan, and making investments. Soon, he had more money, and he bought bigger apartments, and our lifestyle changed. At one point, he was considered to be one of the most wealthy and educated Uyghurs.

During my first two years in the US, it was hard for me to figure out how I could get money. My legal status didn't allow me to work like other people.

For the first year, my dad was able to support me, sending $1000 every month. But it stopped after he was arrested. Then I had no money for rent or for the bi-monthly $2,500 tuition for the English program.

But thankfully, IU still had the money that it was supposed to pay my dad as a visiting scholar. Of course, it was Elliot who dealt with the university and convinced them to give it to me, arguing that since my dad had been arrested on the way for his IU position, the money should be used to support me. Still, that salary was not unlimited—it was only allocated for the fourteen months he was supposed to have been at IU.

I had to learn how to save. My monthly limit was about $1000. That included everything: my insurance, my rent, my food, and the $2,500 fee for school that was due every two months.

I stopped eating fruits and vegetables for a while because they were so expensive. Instead, I relied on chicken drumsticks, potatoes, and onions. And lots of ramen. I gained so much weight because of all the unhealthy food.

At one point, I signed up to be a subject for an optometry school, as part of study for eyedrops. The paid me with a $40 Target gift card; I was able to buy groceries with that.

You know, growing up, I'd lived in a small studio with my entire family, and I'd also lived in a wealthy style. In truth, it was not too hard for me to go back to a frugal lifestyle.

Ensuring Education

Not long before Elliot passed, he convinced the Indiana University administration to give me a merit scholarship, as long as I maintained a 3.5 GPA. It's funny, I don't even know who he talked to; he was never the type to brag or to show off with something like, "You know what I did for you?" He never did stuff like that. Elliot would say something simpler, such as, "I made some phone calls with my connections, and don't worry. You'll be good as long as you study hard." He made it sound easy, but I know he did a lot.

I am forever grateful for that scholarship. How to pay the tuition had been the biggest concern in my head. The rent I could still figure it out. $40,000 per year was not something I could figure out easily. But it was something I knew I needed to make happen.

It was always really important to my father for me to have an education. As a professor, he cared so much about his students. He cared so much about his research, his schoolwork. About learning and being educated.

But here's the thing: I was not a very good student in high school. It's not that I was bad at school; I just didn't like studying. At my boarding school, I preferred dancing and singing. I started a musical club, which included choreography, singing, scriptwriting, and directing. As the president of the club, I became so invested in it. Everybody knew me because all the beautiful girls or the handsome guys were in my club. (I'm just being funny here!) At that point, I was not thinking I would go to study law or Arabic or journalism or political science. I wanted to be a dancer or a singer.

My dad started getting extremely strict, kind of harsh, because he was hoping that I could do really well and then transfer to a high school in the United States or the United Kingdom. Looking back, I think this added pressure to study abroad was due to the police regularly coming to our home. My dad was afraid that my school status would be affected or influenced by the Chinese government. But I couldn't hear it. I was a teenager, and you know how teenagers are: if your parents push you to do something, then you just don't want to do it.

I was kind of being rebellious. *I just want to be a dancer. I just want to be a singer. I just want to do my judo. I just want to be in my band. I want to go to the art school.* I don't think my dad would have been happy to hear me say that. Yeah, he definitely would not have been happy.

But he almost got his way in my second year of high school with a plan to send me to the US. I got my passport. I went to do the visa thing. I was even telling my friends that, "I'm going to leave you guys. I'm gonna miss you guys." I told my best friend since middle school that I was going to go to America soon. *I'm going to miss you.* She was so sad. She even sneaked into my boarding school, climbed the wall, just to say goodbye to me.

But then I ended up staying after the Chinese government blocked my way. They wouldn't allow me to leave the country. I remember my father was so angry at that time—at the Chinese government and me. My dad thought that they found out I was going to go to the US for school because I told my mom about it over the phone. But I don't know for sure how they found out. Maybe they were monitoring our conversations at home.

Two years later, after I'd finished my first semester of university in Beijing, my father decided to take the fellowship in Indiana. When he announced he was taking me for a month, I told that same middle school friend, "Now I'm going to the United States." She didn't take me seriously. "Oh, you said that two years ago."

We didn't really say an official goodbye; after all, I'd be back from Indiana shortly.

We still talk frequently, she and I. Recently, she said, "It's so ridiculous. I never thought that you were really going to leave. But you actually left, and you never came back." She sounded mad. I said, "I had no choice."

Being Watched

Elliot used to describe me as a *mòlìhuā* (茉莉花), which is a delicate jasmine flower. He wanted me to be a *mǔ lǎohǔ* (母老虎), a tough mother tiger.

Indeed, my personality was like a jasmine flower. I was very delicate and scared of things. But also very careful. That was the good part and the bad part. The bad part is that sometimes I wasn't tough enough, but the good part is that I was extremely careful, so afraid to make any mistake, to take any wrong step. I tried very hard not to talk about anything irrelevant or anything that could possibly, even with a tiny little bit of possibility, bring harm to my dad.

In terms of my safety, I was not worried. Being in Bloomington, with everything so familiar, and under Elliot's guardianship, I felt very safe. I figured that I didn't have much to worry about for myself.

My roommate at that time was the one worried that we might have spies breaking into our apartment or trying to assassinate me or something terrible. I'd tell her, "I'm not that important!"

At that point, I had no political agenda at all. No real political views. All I wanted was to talk about my dad. The Chinese government was not so stupid that they would waste their money on a nineteen-year-old girl like me. They might waste it now, but at that time I couldn't imagine it.

Elliot suspected several people of monitoring me at IU. "You should be careful of this person," he'd tell me. "You should be careful of that person. Maybe he is a Chinese spy. Maybe she's a Chinese spy." He was much more cautious than I was. But at IU, many of the Chinese students didn't follow the news at all. In the dance club I was in, there were about eighty Chinese students. None of them read any English news. I'm not joking. *None* of them. Not even one. I don't understand how. Most of them went to the Kelley Business School. Some were in computer science. And none of them cared about politics or human rights.

They had no idea who I was or what had happened to my family.

In all my time at IU, I was only aware of being monitored by one student. The student actually confessed that to me, and then asked me to be careful about what I say because they thought I was a nice person, and they didn't want to have to report on me. The funny thing is that I never noticed being watched until that student told me. But even knowing that, I didn't change my attitude. I said, "I have nothing to hide. It's okay, go report."

Delicate and Scared

Elliot was even careful with Uyghur people. Whenever they called me, Elliot asked me to be extremely cautious and to not become too attached to them. He thought that there might be some Uyghur people trying to use my notoriety or my dad's fame for their own political agenda. So he was quite protective. Extremely protective.

Of course, at that time, there weren't many Uyghur students at Indiana University. Just one visiting scholar and one professor.

I agreed with Elliot. I wanted to keep my distance. I was scared that I would be misunderstood by the Chinese government as having some political agenda, especially a pro-independence one. Because they were accusing my father of being a separatist, I was afraid of being connected to any Uyghur people in the US who might have those views. What if a Uyghur person who approached me was a pro-independence advocate? If I were to be seen with them, or connected to them, the Chinese government could use it as evidence against my entire family.

I was afraid of any possible interactions that could bring more harm to my father or to the rest of the family.

On the one hand, my life would've been so much easier financially and psychologically if I had been in touch with those Uyghur people. I know because they were always offering me so much help. But I had to refuse. As Elliot would always say, we didn't want to give the Chinese authorities any more ammunition to say things like, "That's exactly why we arrested Ilham Tohti. And it's obvious to anyone his daughter went to America just to deal with those pro-independence separatists. That's what Ilham Tohti had planned to do there too."

So I chose to suffer financially (*What am I going to eat? How will I pay next month's rent, my insurance?*) rather than to step into a trap that could possibly harm my dad. I was not willing to risk it at all.

Many of the Uyghur people in the US who reached out were really understanding. They'd say, "We know you're just a scared little girl and that you don't know us."

But there were occasional others who were critical. For example, there was one group in Turkey that accused me of being very Sinicized, Han Chinese style, and they said I clearly didn't like Uyghur people. They said, "You're nothing like your dad."

Even though I didn't know those people and didn't want to care what they thought about me, it was tough to hear them bring up my father. It's critical to remember the important role he had among Uyghur people. He was one of the very first people to introduce Uyghurs to the rest of the world. Without him, the camps might still be unknown, even now. As people in the West were first exposed to what happened to my dad, it began to bring more attention to our community. Slowly, slowly! Reading about him led people to learn more about his arrest, his detention, his trial, his sentence. From there it began to bring in more human rights defenders and advocates and all the awards. And very importantly, my father's public presence allowed the Uyghur people to become more invested in their own plight. After all, they saw their own Uyghur scholar get arrested and sentenced for life. They'd say, "We need to fight for his freedom." Again, this was a slow, slow process.

I give my dad credit for taking part in letting the world know about Uyghurs and how they are treated.

Still, I needed to stay cautious, just like Elliot said. Delicate and scared.

No Visible Lines

While trying to save up money here to support myself, I've also been saving money for my brothers' future college tuition. I wish I could send money for monthly expenses, but it's very difficult. Plus, it makes my family seem more suspicious too. Receiving funds from overseas—especially coming from me—could make problems for them.

There is no visible line for what I can or can't say, in terms of how it will affect my family in China. Everything I say is the truth. There is nothing wrong with it. I just have to try my best to not say anything that the Chinese government can use against my family. Let's say if I just happened to mention the term "East Turkestan" during a talk, the government could decide to take it out of context, and say, "See! She's a separatist!" And then my brothers would be part of *the separatist's family*. That's exactly what they did to my father during his trial.

I'm always aware the Central Government could threaten to deport my brothers from Beijing back to the Uyghur region. My dad and I always wanted my brothers to live in Beijing. At least by being in a city that has more of the international community's attention, my brothers would be less likely to disappear just like that.

So while there may be no visible line, there is a fine line. I can't say anything that gives the authorities any excuse to use my words as evidence against my family. As we've learned, you can't rely on due process or a legal trial or any official rationale. Especially in the Uyghur region, where the laws are different. There, they can disappear you with a snap.

But that doesn't mean I will be silenced, of course.

This might sound cruel and cold blooded, but even if the authorities took away my stepmom's job, and they tried to affect my brothers' student status, I probably would still choose to speak up. It would be so very hard for me and for my brothers. But you know, just as my dad chose to speak for the Uyghur community knowing how it was risking the peace in our family's life, I think I would choose the same too.

In fact, were the Chinese government to go after my family, I promise you I would speak up even stronger. Nothing would hold me back.

Deep Down

Those authorities know who my father is. They know. They'd been monitoring my dad for so long that of course they knew what kind of person my dad really was. They'd sent people to sleep in our homes. To travel with us. Monitor and surveil us. I'm sure they knew my dad was no separatist. I am confident about that. After all that, how could they not know, right?

But they needed him to be in prison and to give him this name of "separatist" to justify their actions. It's obvious to the rest of the world that this was a political message with no real basis. Otherwise, they would've just made all their evidence and the trial public, showing they had total confidence in their case. But deep down they know. They know they are the wrong ones.

The Encyclopedia

Jewher: Every time I had a problem, no matter what type of problem, I could go to Elliot. Help with an editorial in *The New York Times*? Go to Elliot. How to better advocate? Go to Elliot. My friend's dog Arya is not eating. Go to Elliot. I would even go to him if I was sick, asking, "What medicine should I take?" He was—what is the word for the book that has all the answers?

Adam: Encyclopedia?

Jewher: Yes! He was like that for me. Any problem, he always had the answer. And if he didn't have the answer at that moment, he would try to find it and then get back to me. My dad was like that too. But the difference is that Elliot never got mad at me.

Adam: Elliot had Donald Trump to get mad at, not you.

Jewher: Right. But I only bring this up because I think it becomes really important for the next part of my story, to understand that Elliot was not just there to give advice—but he really was, through all these pressures, someone to help me figure things out and learn how to make my way in the world.

Dialogue #1
Tahir Hamut, Poet/Documentarian
Friend of Ilham Tohti
March 2019
Interview originally conducted in Uyghur

Around 1991 I met Ilham Tohti when I was a student at Zhong-yang Minzu University.

مەن ئىلھام توختى بىلەن1991 -يىللىرى ئەتراپىدا مەركىزىي مىللەتلەر ئۇنۋېرستېتىدا ئوقۇغۇچى ۋاقتىمدا كۆرۈشكەن.

At that time, he'd recently come to Minzu University as a master's student after graduating from Northeastern University.

ئۇ چاغدا ئىلھام شەرقىي شىمال ئۇنۋېرستېتىنى پۈتتۈرۈپ مەركىزىي مىللەتلەر ئۇنۋېرستېتىغا يېڭى كەلگەن ۋاقتى ئىدى.

His research focus and main interest was on the Uyghur population, most enthusiastically looking at the Uyghur economy and its development.

ئىلھامنىڭ ئەينى چاغدىكى ئاساسلىق تەتقىقات نىشانى ۋە قىزىقىش نۇقتىسى ئۇيغۇرلارنىڭ نوپۇس مەسلىسى ھەم ئىقتىسادىي تەرەققىيات ئەھۋالى ئىدى.

It was our frequent topic of conversation when we were together, when he would share his opinions about the state of Uyghur language, culture, and education.

مۇشۇ توغرىۋلۇق بىز جىق پاراڭلىشاتتۇق. ئاندىن كېيىن ئۇيغۇرلارنىڭ ماائارىپ، تىل ۋە مەدەنىيەت ئىشلىرىغىمۇ ئۆزىنىڭ كۆز قاراشلىرىنى دەيتتى.

53

He never stopped working to find the best solutions for solving the problems that Uyghurs faced. Ilham cared so much about his people. He was so worried for them.

ئۇ توختىماي ئىزدىنىپ ئۇيغۇرلار دۇچ كېلىۋاتقان مەسىلىلەرنىڭ
چارىسىنى ۋە ياخشى بىر يولىنى تېپىشقا تىرىشاتتى. ئىلھام ئۆز
خەلقىگە شۇنچىلىك كۆڭۈل بۆلەتتى ۋە ئۇلارنىڭ غېمىنى يەيتتى.

That period left such a deep influence on me.

ئىلھام بىلەن تونۇشقان شۇ چاغلار ماڭا ئىنتايىن چوڭقۇر تەسىر
قالدۇرغان ئىدى.

*   *   *

I'd studied Uyghur literature in Zhongyang Minzu University in 1987. In between spring and summer of 1989, the University students in Beijing began to demonstrate and show their discontent concerning some of the CCP's policies.

مەن 1987-يىلى مەركىزى مىللەتلەر ئىنىستىتۇتىنىڭ ئۇيغۇر
تىلى ئەدەبىيات كەسپىگە ئوقۇشقا بارغان. 1989-يىلى باھار
ۋە ياز مەزگىلىدە بېيجىڭدىكى ئالىي مەكتەپ
ئوقۇغۇچىلىرىنىڭ ئېينى چاغدىكى جۇڭگوكومپارتىيەسىنىڭ
بەزى سىياسەتلىرىگە ئۆزىنىڭ نارازىلىقىنى ئىپادىلەشكە
باشلىغان شۇ ۋاقىتلارغا شاھىت بولدۇم.

They expressed their desire for democracy and progress by demonstrating on the streets. And they went on strike from school.

ئوقۇغۇچىلار ئۆزىنىڭ دېموكراتىيەگە ۋە ئىسلاھاتقا بولغان
ئارزۇلىرىنى ئىپادىلەپ كوچىغا چىقىپ نامايىش قىلىپ دەرس
تاشلاشقا باشلىغان ئىدى.

At that time, there were at least five to six hundred Uyghur students in this university—undergraduates, graduate students, art students, some who there for special training, and adults who came for continuing education.

شۇ چاغدا مەركىزىي مىللەتلەر ئونۇۋېرستېتىدا 600–500
ئۇيغۇر ئوقۇغۇچىلار بولۇپ، بۇنىڭ ئىچىدە ئاسپىراتلىقتا
باكلاۋۇرلۇقتا ۋە باشقا ھەرخىل كەسپلەردە ئوقۇۋاتقانلار،
ئوتتۇرا تېخنىكوم ئوقۇغۇچىلىرى، تەربىيلىنىشكە كەلگەنلەر
بولۇپ خېلى سالماقنى ئىگەللەيتى.

As Uyghur students, we discussed whether or not we should attend the student movement.

شۇ چاغدا بىز ئۇيغۇرلارئىچىدە بولۇۋاتقان
ئوقۇغۇچىلار ھەرىكەتىگە قاتنىشامدۇق قاتناشمامدۇق
دېگەن مەسىلىدە ئارىمىزدا ئويلىنىش بولدى.

Out of that came two kinds of opinions . . .

ۋە بۇنىڭغا قارىتا ئىككى خىل پىكىر چۇشتى.

. . . one of them thought that it was the Chinese students' movement, so they didn't care about it, preferring to just keep going with their classes . . .

بەزىلەر «بۇ خەنزۇلارنىڭ ئۆزىنىڭ ئىشى، بىز بۇنىڭغا نېمە
قىلمىز ئارىلىشىپ، بىز دەرسنى تاشلىمايلى،
دەرسىمىزنى داۋاملاشتۇرىۋەرەيلى» دېدى.

. . . and others thought that if China were to become a progressive democracy with better policies, then it would be better for Uyghurs—a perspective seen as strongly related to our destiny.

يەنە بىر تۈركۈم ئۇيغۇرچىلار جۇڭگونىڭ دىموكراتىيەگە
مېڭىشى، ئىسال ھاتقا يول ئېلىشى، جۇڭگو ۋەزىيتىننىڭ
ياخشلىنىشى ئۇيغۇرلارغىمۇ ياخشى، بۇ بىزنىڭ تەقدىرىمىز
بىلەن مۇناسۋەتلىك دېدى.

So we decided to add our voice to the democracy movement, standing up for a free and developing China.

شۇڭا بىز جۇڭگۇنىڭ دىموكراتىيە لىشىشگە، ئەركىن
بولۇشىغا ۋە تەرە ققى قىلىشىغا بىزمۇ ئاۋازىمىزنى
چىقارمساق بولمايدۇ دېگەن قارارغا كەلدۇق.

I was one of them, a very active organizer and leader of Uyghur students in this movement.

مەن بۇ جەريانىدا ئىزچىل تۈردە مەركىزىي مىللەتلەر
ئۇنۋۇپرستىتىدكى شنجاڭلىق ئۇقۇغۇچىلارنىڭ
تەشكىللىگۈچىسى ۋە يتەكلىگۈچىسىننىڭ بىرى سۈپىتىدە بۇ
پائالىيەتلەرگە ئاكتىپ قاتناشتىم.

In May, at Tiananmen Square, the Chinese students went on a hunger strike. We did it too.

5-ئايغا كەلگەن چاغدا تىيەنئەنمىن مەيدانىدا خەنزۇ
ئۇقۇغۇچىلارنىڭ تاماق تاشلاش ھەركىتى باشلاندى. بىزمۇ
ئاۋاز قوۋشۇپ تاماق تاشلدۇق.

But on the Fourth of June, the students' movement was stopped by a massacre from the Chinese People's Liberation Army.

كېيىن ئۇقۇغۇچىلار ھەركىتى 6-ئاينىڭ 4-كۈنى ئازاتلىق
ئارمىيە تەرپىدىن قانلىق باستۇرۇلدى.

56

Because I went on a hunger strike for seven days, I was in bad health. From my bed in the school's hospital, all day along I heard the gun shots. The next day they brought a lot of students' corpses by truck to the school.

6-ئاينىڭ 4-كۈنى ھەربىيلەر تيەنئەنمىن مەيدانىغا كىرىپ ئوقۇغۇچىلارنى ئېتىشقا باشلىغاندا، مەن يەتتە كۈن تاماق تاشلىۋاتقانچقا، سالامە تلكىم ياخشى بولماي مەكتەپنىڭ ئامبۇلاتورىيسسىدە ياتاقتا يېتىپتۇئاتقان ئىدىم. ياتاقنىڭ سىرتىدىن ئوق ئاۋازىنى ئاڭلاپ تۇردۇق. ئەتىسى نۇرغۇن ئۆلگەن ئادەملەرنىڭ جەسسەتلىرىنى ماشىنلارغا بېسىپ مەكتەپلەرگە ئەكەلدى.

So many students were killed. So many of them disappeared. It was so sad. A tragic outcome for the whole world.

نۇرغۇن ئوقۇغۇچىلار ئۆلدى. نۇرغۇن ئادەم يوقاپ كەتتى. بۇ ناھايىتى ئىچىنىشلىق بىر ۋەقە بولدى. پۈتكۈل دۇنياغا نىسبەتەن زور بىر قىرغىنچىلىق بولدى.

From there, we were left with a big question of what we should do.

بۇ ئىش بىزنىمۇ ھەم قانداق قىلىشمىز كېرەك دېگەن سۆئال ئۈستىدە ئويلاندۇرۇپ قويىدى.

What would China choose?

جۇڭگو قايسى يولنى تاللايدۇ؟

What would be the destiny of Uyghurs?

ئۇيغۇرلارنىڭ تەقدىرى قانداق بولىدۇ؟

*　　　　*　　　　*

At the beginning of 2014, we heard that Ilham was detained in Beijing.

2014-يىلنىڭ بېشىدا ئىلھامنىڭ بېيجىڭدا تۇتقۇن قىلىنغانلىقىنى ئاڭلىدۇق.

I was astounded because his way of solving problems on behalf of Uyghur rights was always to work within the laws of China. So there wasn't any legal reason to arrest him.

بۇنى ئاڭلاپ بەكلا ھەيران قالدىم. چۈنكى ئىلھامنىڭ ئۇيغۇرلارنىڭ ھەق-ھوقۇقىنى قوغداش ئۈچۈن تۇتقان يولى ئىزچىل جۇڭگۇنىڭ قانۇن دائىرىسىدە بولغان. شۇڭا ئۇنى تۇتۇپ كېتىشنىڭ ھىچقانداق قانۇنىي ئاساسى يوق ئىدى.

I knew the police harassed him frequently, especially if he were involved in any big activities or international meetings, or if some well-known foreigners were coming to visit him in Beijing. The police would take Ilham far away to cut off all communications.

ئۈنىڭدىن بۇرۇن ئىلھامنىڭ نەچچە قېتىم ساقچىلار تەرىپىدىن ئاۋارە قىلىنغانلىقىنى بىلە تتىم. بولۇپمۇ ئۇ بېيجىڭدا يۈز بەرگەن بىرەرچوڭ پائالىيەتلەرگە قاتناشسا ياكى چەتئەللىك كىشىلەر ئۇنى يوقلاپ قالسا ساقچىلار ئۇنى ئىزدەيتتى. ئىلھامنى »چاي ئىچىش« كە تەكلىپ قىلىپ ياكى ئۇياق-بۇياقلارغا ئېلىپ كېتىپ، ھېچكىم بىلەن ئالاقە قىلدۇرمايتتى.

But this last time was terrible news.

ئەمما بۇ قېتىم قولغا ئېلىنىشى ماڭا نىسبەتەن بەك چوڭ شۇم خەۋەر بولدى.

Intellectuals and friends of his in Ürümqi gathered immediately to discuss his arrest.

بـز ئۇرۇمچىدىكى ئۆقۇمۇشلۇق تونۇش-بىلىشلەر، ئىلھامنىڭ دوستلىرى قاتارلىقلار بۇ ئۇچۇرنى ئاڭلاپلا دەرھال يىغىلىپ قانداق قىلىشىمىز كېرەكلىكى توغرۇلۇق مەسلىھەت قىلىشتۇق.

After searching to find out which bureau arrested him, we learned that it was the Public Security Bureau of the city of Ürümqi.

ئۇنى قايسى ئورگاننىڭ تۇتقانلىقىنى سۈرۈشتە قىلىپ ئۇرۇمچى شەھەرلىك جامائەت خەۋپسىزلىك ئىدارىسىدىنڭ تۇتۇپ كەتكەنلىكنى بىلدۇق.

That discovery shocked us most—to learn that it was possible that the police in Ürümqi could arrest a university professor who worked and lived in Beijing.

بۇ بىزنى تېخىمۇ چۆچۈتۈۋەتتى. قانداق دىگەندە، ئۇرۇمچى شە ھەرىدىن ساقچى بېرىپ بېيجىڭدا ئىشلەيدىغان ئالىي مەكتەپنىڭ پروفېسسورىنى تۇتۇپ كەلگىنى بىزنى ھەيران قالدۇردى.

That was something that we'd never considered.

بۇ بىز بۇرۇن ئويلاپمۇ باقمىغان ئىش.

There were no rules or regulations in the Chinese constitution that fit that scenario.

ھەم جۇڭگونىڭ ئاساسى قانۇنى، ئەدلىيە سىستىممىسىدىمۇ ئۇنداق تەرتىپ يوق ئىدى.

It was the sign of a worsening situation.

دېمەك بۇ ئەھۋالنىڭ تېخىمۇ ناچارلىشىپ كېتىۋاتقانلىقىنىڭ
بىشارىتى ئىدى.

*   *   *

It was impossible that the police from Ürümqi would arrest someone from Beijing unless the decision came from Central Committee of the CCP. In other words, it was the first step of heavy oppression.

ئەگەر مەركىزىي كومىتېتىنىڭ بۇيرۇقى بولمىسا ئۈرۈمچىنىڭ
ساقچىسى بېرىپ بېيجىڭدىن بىر ئادەمنى تۆتالمايدۇ.
مۇنداقچە قىلىپ ئېيتقاندا بۇ ئىش ئۇيغۇرلارنىڭ بېشىغا
كېلىۋاتقان ئاپەتنىڭ بىرىنچى قەدىمى ئىدى.

Immediately, we began to delete some articles on our computers. We knew the CCP's investigation would reach us soon too.

شۇنىڭ بىلەن بىز دەرھال كومپيۇتېرلىرىمىزدىكى بەزى
ماقالىلەرنى ئۆچۈرۈشكە باشلىدۇق. چۈنكى ئىلھامنىڭ بېشىغا
كەلگەن كۈن تېزلا بىزنىڭمۇ بېشىمىزغا كېلىشى مۇمكىن
ئىدى.

Not long after that, on May 5th, the State Security Department of Ürümqi came to me.

ئۇزۇن ئۆتمەيلا، يەنى 5-ئاينىڭ 5-كۈنى، ئۈرۈمچى شەھەرلىك
دۆلەت خەۋپسىزلىك ئىدارىسىدىن مېنى ئىزدەپ كەلدى.

They asked me what kind of relationship I had with Ilham Tohti.

سېنىڭ ئىلھام بىلەن قانداق مۇناسىۋىتىڭ بار، دەپ سورىدى.

I said that we were in once at the same school, and that we were good friends, and that we were in touch from time to time.

ئىلھام بىلەن بىز ئەينى چاغدا دوست بولۇپ ياخشى ئۆتكەن.
پات ـ پات ئالاقىلىشىپ تۇرىمىز دەپ جاۋاپ بەردىم.

They left after some more questioning.

ھە، دەپ ئەھۋالنى ئىگەللەپ قايتىپ كەتتى.

That June we learned that that he was officially arrested, and in September he was sentenced to life in prison.

ئاندىن كېيىن ئىلغامنىڭ 6-ئايدا رەسمىي قولغا ئېلىنغىنىنى،
9-ئايدا مۇددەتسىز قاماققا ھۆكۈم قىلىنغانلىقىنى ئاڭلىدۇق.

The verdict was truly sad and shocking . . .

بۇنىڭدىن كۆڭلىمىز ھەقىقەتەن بەك يېرىم بولدى،
چۆچۈپ كەتتۇق.

. . . because his penalty was, overall, a signal to all Uyghur intel-lectuals.

چۈنكى ئىلھامنىڭ بۇنداق بىر تەرەپ قىلىنىشى پۈتكۈل ئۇيغۇر
زىيالىيلىرىغا بېرىلگەن بىر سىگنال ئىدى.

It would set the main trend for Uyghurs.

ئۇيغۇرلارنىڭ تەقدىرىنىڭ يۆنىلىشىدىن بىشارەت بېرەتتى.

From that point forward, we would live in anxiety and fear.

شۇنىڭدىن تارتىپ بىز ئىزچىل تۈردە تەشۋىش ۋە ۋەھىمە
ئىچىدە قالدۇق.

PART THREE
Dark Days

A Premonition

It might sound a little superstitious, I don't know. It was a Friday. At the time, Elliot still hadn't been found. He was in New York; I was in Bloomington. My Uyghur instructor at IU, Professor Gulnisa, invited me to her house for dinner. I'd been to her place multiple times and didn't think twice when I punched in the address for Uber. Sitting in the backseat of the car, I was playing on my phone, not paying attention to where we were going. But when we arrived, I realized I was somewhere that at the same time was very unfamiliar *and* familiar.

I told the Uber driver that something was wrong. "This is not Professor Gulnisa's house." He checked his dashboard and then looked up at me in the rear-view mirror. "This is where the GPS led me."

Only then did I realize we were at Elliot's old house.

Had I accidentally copy-pasted Elliot's address into the Uber?

Later, once I got home, I called Elliot because I wanted to ask him, "You know what happened today?"

But he didn't pick up.

I texted him, "Hello!" But he didn't respond.

I was so confused. He was always immediately responsive. I'd seen him in New York just two or three weeks earlier. I was wondering: *Did I do anything that pissed him off? Did he get mad because I hadn't contacted him over the past week?* My dad could be like that too. He could ignore me for a while if he got mad at me. So I was thinking maybe that was the case with Elliot right now. I was like, "Okay, fine."

The next day our mutual friend, Yaxue, called me. In 2016, the three of us had travelled to Europe to lobby at the European Parliament for my dad to be nominated for the Sakharov Prize. Yaxue said, "I've been trying to get in touch with Elliot for few days. He's not responding."

"Same for me," I said. "Elliot never does that." My heart began jumping so fast. People not responding to each other for a day or even a week might be normal, but it was absolutely not normal for Elliot and me. He'd always respond within two minutes. It was like he was waiting for my text message.

I told Yaxue I was going to call Elliot's daughter, Coline.

News

"Jewher, I know this is going to be very hard for you to hear."

"What is happening? Is Elliot sick?"

"Dad passed away."

My mom was with me at that time, as well as another guest. It was January, during the Spring Festival. So with twenty days off from work, my mom had come for a rare winter visit.

I just froze on the phone call. I didn't know how to react. I immediately started crying nonstop.

Coline sounded really calm at that time. "Jewher, I know it's going to be very hard for you, but don't worry. I will always support you just like how Dad did." Imagine, she was trying to comfort *me* when it was *her* father who passed away.

"No," I said. "This is not about if I have anyone to support me." And then I asked if she was doing okay.

Honestly, I just could not process the information. I wanted to think she was joking. But I know a daughter would never say anything like that about her father.

Discovery

Elliot was found at his apartment in Jackson Heights. He was supposed to be at a conference speaking. When he didn't show up, friends and colleagues were calling and calling him, but he didn't pick up. Everybody was looking for him. Finally the apartment management went and opened the door and discovered Elliot. There were some people who suspected that the Chinese government had assassinated him. But following the autopsy, the doctor said he had passed away from a sudden heart attack.

He'd retired just two years earlier in 2015. Elliot had always talked about wanting to leave Indiana for his native New York. He'd bought an apartment in Queens and for years had slowly been moving his stuff there.

Although I hadn't wanted him to leave Bloomington, I also knew that I was not the center of the world; I couldn't expect everyone to turn around me all the time. But Elliot said not to worry, we'd always see each other. Just not in Indiana. He said, "I'm not coming back here! But you can come to visit me."

After he moved, we Skyped almost every single day. Just like how I'd done with my dad in the past. And even when we didn't talk *every* single day, we would make sure to text.

And I still saw him often. If I was traveling to DC, he would come down there to see me. Or if I had to be in New York for a day, he would take the subway all the way from Queens to Manhattan just to be with me. In fact, the last time I saw him was when he took a 7 a.m. train into Manhattan just to drop me off at the United Nations. It was like a dad who drops his daughter off at her kindergarten. He saw me enter, and then he left.

Finding a Way Home

In Uyghur culture, when a loved one dies, we make a type of pastry called koymak. One whose smell is strong and lasts a long time. You deep fry the dough and press it in sugar. Then you open the windows so the ghost of your loved ones can smell it and find their way home. It takes lots of time to make.

Almost right away, we started cooking, my mom and I, readying them for a memorial going on in New York the next morning. My guest, knowing how much this was affecting me, left early. He didn't want to be in the way.

All night we baked. Barely slept.

Knowing lots of people would come to the service, we cooked enough for everyone. Two giant pans. And we carried them with us though the airport at 6 a.m. the next morning.

6 a.m.

It was such an awful and confusing time. I felt like everyone was leaving me. My roommate left me. Elliot left me. I had no contact with my dad, or even any information about him. I was really lonely, and I felt as if this were the end. So when this happened, it was so great that my mom happened to be there. Usually she comes for summer, but that was the first time she'd come during winter. There are so many coincidences in my life. It often feels like the exact moment when I need someone, there's always someone there.

The reason we picked the 6 a.m. flight was because it was the cheapest one. It was not the direct flight. Even still, we had a hard time affording it. I really struggled with money at that time, always worrying about paying bills. And my mom's salary was enough for her in China, but not enough to buy last minute airline tickets. She'd need to use her entire month's salary. But at that moment our thinking was: *Don't worry about money. Just go. We will think about how to pay the rent after we come back.*

I cried the whole time on the airplane. My face was swollen; my eyes were swollen. Usually, I always wear makeup when I'm outside. But today, I didn't care how I looked. For the entire flight, my mom just kept hugging me and patting me. She understood how much Elliot meant to me, how he'd filled in that empty spot where neither of my parents had been able to be when I'd first arrived in the US.

Memorial Service

The memorial was initiated by Tibetan people in New York, due to Elliot's prominent research, studies, and deep connections to that community. When I saw Coline there, I cried so hard. She is few years older than me, but so much more mature than me. Do you remember when I said that after my dad was sentenced to life, I couldn't accept anyone's phone call? How I disappeared for a few days because I couldn't process any of it? How I did not want to talk to people about it? Well, Coline had to inform Elliot's friends and students and professors. She had to host this ceremony. How hard it must have been for her.

There were about fifty to eighty people in the room, mostly Tibetans. I sat in back with my mom. When I saw cameras, I told my mom, "Don't raise your head." Even though she was here for me, she did need to be concerned about being seen with Tibetans. I said, "Just look down like this so the camera won't see you."

Everyone was given a small Buddhist book of prayers to say aloud. But I couldn't understand it because it was written in Tibetan. So instead, in Arabic, I recited from the Qur'an. Ever since my mom moved to Beijing, she hasn't closely practiced Islam. She hasn't said her prayers for years, but there she was, also doing it with me. Hearing her was comforting because I was feeling such intense sorrow and deep pain.

Next, they invited people to get up to say some words to memorialize Elliot, starting with Coline. It was so moving to hear how much Elliot meant to so many people. I just wanted to sit and listen.

Then someone asked, "Jewher, would you like to come up?"

I made my way up in front of all these people whom Elliot had touched. I only made it through one sentence, before I managed to say through my tears that I was sorry, that I wasn't able to talk. I was just crying so hard. And then my mom, forgetting about being away from the cameras, rushed up and hugged me in front of everyone. And Coline came up too. The three of us, we just hugged each other and cried.

Elliot: my mentor, protector, and uncle.

An Uncle

There is a photo of Elliot that they gave us at the memorial. It hangs in front of my bed. Every day I see his picture.

Elliot was nice to everyone. Yes, he was always sarcastic and tried to act like he was mean, but everyone knew he had the purest heart.

I always said he was like my uncle. And while I did not replace my dad with him, I put him in the same place as my dad. He tried everything he could do to make me not feel alone in the US.

Elliot gave me all the possible love one could ever give to a stranger.

Chills

I was having a private one-to-one class with Professor Gulnisa in her office. It wasn't long after Elliot had passed. I spaced out while she was saying something. Suddenly I heard Elliot's voice, saying, "No, Jewher, pay attention. Pay attention. You have to be a good student." I immediately got chills.

"Oh, my god," I said out loud, a shiver running down my back.

That was the only time that happened though. That was the only time. I think Elliot might have been there.

Giving Up

When he first passed away, I almost gave up on advocacy work. I was not motivated at all. I just rejected everything. Interviews. Offers to speak. I told myself that I'm just going to study. Focus on school.

For almost for a year, I was down. I was not doing well at all.

It just felt like everything was out of my control. I couldn't save anyone. Everyone that I cared about was not around me anymore. And I felt kind of abandoned. It seemed like everything was going wrong. Everything. And I thought that maybe this was God's plan. That I'm not supposed to get anything I wanted in my life. I was self-denying for everything.

And I questioned whether anything I'd done for my dad had mattered. The Chinese government had prevented any family visits with him, meaning we had no information on his condition. And I just started believing that nothing was helping. That everything was just going downhill. And I couldn't shake the feeling that all the advocacy work was not worth much at all.

And with Elliot gone, it felt as though there was nobody there to guide me. What was I going to do? What if I made a bad decision? I'd have to be responsible for all the bad decisions I might make.

The most I usually did to reduce my pressure was to dance. I danced so much. After Elliot passed in January, I tried to keep practicing for the biggest dance performance of our club that was scheduled to happen in February. I was supposed to perform as one of the central dancers. But I just couldn't do it. I said, "I don't think this is the right time to perform." My teammates in the dance club tried to convince me to continue, saying that "Your uncle would not be happy if he saw you not dancing." I said, "I just can't do it now. This is my way of showing respect." I did not go back to dancing for quite some time, maybe eight or nine months later.

The best I can say is that I did focus on school, burying myself in the library almost all the time. But other than that, I was not motivated. I'd just get too emotional about everything.

It was best to just close down for a while.

A Bad Year

Adam: Without making you have to relive all this, it sounds as though during that time all the things that normally gave you comfort and purpose weren't there. Advocacy, dance, religion, even friends. You truly felt alone, Yes?

Jewher: Yeah, 2017 was really a bad year.

Adam: I'm sorry.

Jewher: A really bad year for me.

Sometimes

For a while, I'd call Elliot's phone number to hear his voicemail. To pretend like he was going to pick it up.

One afternoon, between the writing of this book and my work, I found myself particularly stressed and lost. I texted Elliot just to find comfort. Imagine my shock when I saw the three little dots that indicate a reply is being written. For a moment, I was so spooked, thinking he might actually be responding to me. Was it possible? As it turned out, someone else now had his phone number. But amazingly that person answered with kindness and understanding, even saying I should always feel free to write back if it helps me to feel better.

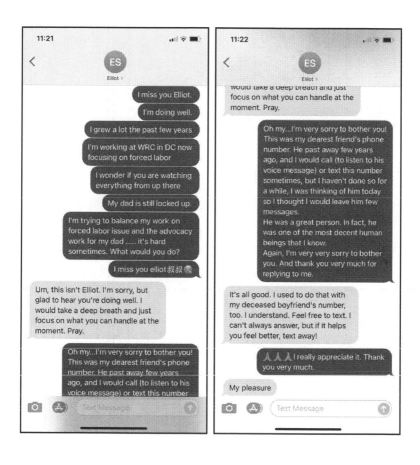

Left screen:

11:21

ES
Elliot >

I miss you Elliot.

I'm doing well.

I grew a lot the past few years

I'm working at WRC in DC now focusing on forced labor

I wonder if you are watching everything from up there

My dad is still locked up.

I'm trying to balance my work on forced labor issue and the advocacy work for my dad ..... it's hard sometimes. What would you do?

I miss you elliot 叔叔😢

Um, this isn't Elliot. I'm sorry, but glad to hear you're doing well. I would take a deep breath and just focus on what you can handle at the moment. Pray.

Oh my...I'm very sorry to bother you! This was my dearest friend's phone number. He past away few years ago, and I would call (to listen to his voice message) or text this number

Right screen:

11:22

ES
Elliot >

would take a deep breath and just focus on what you can handle at the moment. Pray.

Oh my...I'm very sorry to bother you! This was my dearest friend's phone number. He past away few years ago, and I would call (to listen to his voice message) or text this number sometimes, but I haven't done so for a while, I was thinking of him today so I thought I would leave him few messages.
He was a great person. In fact, he was one of the most decent human beings that I know.
Again, I'm very very sorry to bother you. And thank you very much for replying to me.

It's all good. I used to do that with my deceased boyfriend's number, too. I understand. Feel free to text. I can't always answer, but if it helps you feel better, text away!

🙏🙏🙏 I really appreciate it. Thank you very much.

My pleasure

79

PART 4

A Genocide

Slowly, Slowly

My stepmom started saying that they were afraid to go back to the Uyghur region. In the past, my family would go to spend the summer with our relatives. This was usually no big deal. But now, without her getting into much detail, just the thought of it seemed to bring her a lot of concern.

Later, I couldn't stop thinking about it. I kept wondering: *Why is she scared to go?*

Slowly, slowly, throughout 2017, I started hearing more and more about people disappearing. I heard this person got arrested. That person got arrested.

We heard it on the news. From Uyghur people posting on social media. We just heard all kinds of things.

But we didn't have the concept of concentration camps yet. We just knew that more and more people were disappearing.

We started to get some word of what was happening after a few Kazakhs and Kyrgyz were able to get released. In most cases, they'd been in the Uyghur region and had gotten arrested accidentally. And obviously China couldn't arrest people from other countries, so they had to release them. Other times, people were released because they were married to foreign nationals. That opened the door for people to hear what they'd been through and how many people were being held. That was the time the concept of *lagér* (لاگېر)—which means "camp" in Uyghur language—started to enter people's minds.

That word didn't make sense to me at that point. What is a camp? I didn't have a context for it. The only meaning I knew of the word "camp" was in reference to going camping. I learned more when I started looking up the term and began to understand it in terms of history. It took some time to process. Could things really have gotten that bad?

I still had some doubts. Is it really true? That bad? Could there really be that many people interned there? Is it really a concentration camp?

My dad had been disappeared multiple times over the years, and each time he got put on house arrest and then would be released again. I thought maybe the same thing was happening to others. Maybe people who were like my dad, who could get a little political, who criticized the government, were the ones being arrested. But the more testimonies I heard, the more news I read, I realized it was not only happening to intellectuals. Almost any Uyghur in the region could be sent to a camp or a prison.

I didn't want to believe it. Because in my mind, I wanted to believe China was still a peaceful country. I was holding onto the idea that most of the Chinese people whom I knew were really kind. That they wouldn't do such things to others. I couldn't make sense of how the government thought it was okay to do things like this to such a large group of people and expect the citizenry to go along with it.

I know Uyghurs historically have been under persecution. But it was never at this level in my lifetime. I just couldn't imagine that the Chinese government would start a targeting campaign at this scale. But as it turned out, they did and still continue to do so.

Basically, as long as you are an ethnic minority in the Uyghur region, especially Uyghur, then you can be considered a criminall. The PRC introduced terms such as "separatist" and "extremist" into the Chinese conversations about Uyghurs to justify the repression of Uyghur intellectuals like my father who they thought raised too many questions. But I didn't think they would do things like that to any random person.

So I totally got it when my Han Chinese friends did not accept it when I told them about what was happening in the Uyghur region or when they read about it. They assumed it was all Western propaganda. Even as a Uyghur who had experienced the severity of the Chinese authorities, I needed some time to process this information. It was easy to understand why those Chinese students or Chinese people could deny the existence of the camps.

The Film

Initially, my role in the documentary was supposed to only include a storyline about my dad. The film itself, about human rights in China, was going to focus on a few key areas: the protests in Tiananmen Square, the crackdown on human rights lawyers, and then the story of the Uyghurs.

But after the producer interviewed me, he asked if he could make me the main storyline of the Uyghur stories—especially when he saw that my father was a thread between all the main points—he'd been a student in Beijing during the Tiananmen massacre, his own lawyer (a Han Chinese human rights lawyer) had been arrested, and, of course, he'd been China's primary example of what can happen to Uyghurs who are too vocal. That was going to be the main focus. But when news about the camps started coming out, we understood that we were not going to just talk about my father anymore. We were looking at a persecution of an entire culture and population—the largest mass detention of an ethno-religous group since World War II. And we wanted to hear more firsthand accounts of what was happening in the camps. It needed to be documented.

It was crazy how fast things escalated. None of us expected it.

On camera, I heard testimony from a Uyghur woman who had escaped the camps. Mihrigul Tursun was married to an Egyptian man whom she met in Cairo while studying for her master's degree. Together, she and her husband had triplets, and her troubles began when she brought the newborns back to the Uyghur region to meet their grandparents. The babies were very tiny, just a few months old. But immediately, when she arrived at the airport, she was shackled and had a black sack placed over on her head. She and her children were taken away but sent to different places. Mihrigul was detained for about nine months. At one point, she was released for a little bit, only to be sent back again.

She has beautiful blue eyes and brown hair—something you see with some Uyghurs. She was so skinny when she got released. She told me she was not able to eat. They'd given her rotten food, and they would only give her water around once a week. And the water was not even clean. It looked milky and dirty. But they still had to drink it because that was the *only* water they could access. Otherwise they would die. The reason she said the guards gave her water was because the female prisoners needed to take a type of medicine. To this day, she still doesn't know what that medicine was. But she had to take it. It made her dizzy and weak, and she stopped menstruating. This was true for all those around her.

All of the women were naked, about thirty or forty in one tiny room. Often beaten and tortured. At night when they wanted to sleep, the women didn't have enough space to lie down next to each other. So twenty people would stand against the wall, and every two hours, they would take turns trying to sleep. They weren't allowed to take showers, and without bathrooms, they had to relieve themselves in the cells. Everyone got sick; it was so unhygienic.

Because her babies had Egyptian passports, Mihrigul's husband was able to involve the Egyptian embassy. It resulted in her release, sort of. The Chinese authorities told her she could escort her triplets back to her husband's family in Egypt, but then she had to immediately return to the Uyghur region. They threatened to arrest her parents and her siblings if she didn't.

Mihrigul agreed. What else could she do?

Before her release, she was forced to put on makeup and do a video saying that she'd never been tortured while being detained. Never beaten. That she'd only come to the camps to learn, and that she was doing well. She then was taken to a hospital to retrieve her babies. But by then, the mother of triplets was now a mother of twins. The third one had died while in custody. There were visible wounds across his neck.

After Mihrigul's husband went to China to look for her, he disappeared as well. And he's Egyptian! That really got her thinking. How could she return to China, as she promised she would, after bringing the babies back to Egypt? Who could she even drop them with in Egypt, since her husband was not there anymore? Plus, after her husband disappeared, would she really be any safer in Egypt? That was when she made her decision, one that no one should have to make.

Mihrigul ran to the American Embassy. "I felt so sorry to my parents," she said. "They raised me. They raised me with care and love, but I had to betray them like that for my own children."

The Embassy arranged for her and the babies' passage to the US. For the first few months, the FBI was protecting her. She was scared. People she assumed to be Chinese nationals threw stones at her window. She would have panic attacks and have to contact the FBI. Over the first few months that Mihrigul stayed in the US, she transferred apartments a few times. Because she just never felt safe.

When I interviewed Mihrigul, I couldn't even continue asking all of the questions. (One of the producers had written down the ones that he wanted me to ask.) She was crying and yelling as she told her story. I didn't even know what facial expression I should put on, or how to express how sorry I was.

I didn't even know how to comfort her. I didn't know where to put my hands. Should I hold her? Should I hug her? Because she was just shaking. She couldn't control herself. And I felt so terrible. I just wanted to help her to feel better, but I didn't know how.

Look, I already feel terrible enough that my father was sent to prison. Imagine, her own baby was killed. How devastated she must have felt. How could anyone, *anyone*, harm a baby?

Mihrigul's testimony brought out a higher feeling of outrage in me.

I was so mad. I was so, so, so angry. Both of my hands were trembling. After Elliot died, I'd lost my motivation. I was just trying to get through school. Now, after hearing what happened to Mihrigul, I made a promise to myself: I am going to really fight this. Nothing will stop me.

Testifying before the Congressional-Executive Commission on China in 2018.

Boiling Frogs

I knew the persecution of Uyghurs was happening—it was not a recent thing. It's been happening for decades. But slowly. In Chinese, there's a saying: *Wēnshuǐ zhǔ qīngwā* (温水煮青蛙). It suggests using warm water to start boiling frogs. The frogs don't even know they are under threat until they realize the water is boiling hot, and then they can't escape anymore. And now we Uyghurs are in the boiling hot water period of time. In the past, we all thought it was okay, things were just getting a little warm. We were going to be fine. And slowly, the heat turned up, bit by bit, but still we thought we could handle it. And now it's burning hot. It's killing every frog in that pot.

Until about 2018, I was not in touch with many Uyghurs, other than those with whom I was in contact in relation to advocacy for my dad. As the detentions and disappearances escalated, many Uyghurs would reach out to me on social media, asking if they could have my number. It was very common to hear, "I don't feel safe talking over Instagram." When eventually we'd talk, they'd tell me, "I really don't know where to start. You have reached the highest level of attention for your father's case. Would you give me some advice?" I would receive pictures of their family members, along with the family members' identification numbers and full names and the dates when they were arrested. They were just looking for anyone they could contact for help. I would introduce them to certain people I knew in government in Washington, DC. Additionally, some people I knew established a database of the missing and detained Uyghurs. I helped teach some people how to enter their missing family members into the database with the hope that they would teach someone else, and on down the line, until eventually everybody knew how to do it.

Being connected to this nearly every day reinforced to me how big the problem was, how hot the water was boiling. And I wanted the world to hear their stories. I wanted to interview more camp survivors and family members of people who had been sent to camps or prisons.

This is the reality: every Uyghur friend I have on social media has at least one—and often up to ten—family members who have been locked up. Literally *every* one of them. And I have at least a thousand friends on social media. For so many years, I felt alone with what happened to my dad, as though nobody could really and truly understand what I was going through. But now, everyone understands. We're all in this together. It's sad that I don't feel alone anymore. Honestly, I would rather feel alone again because that would mean nobody would have to suffer what I've suffered.

Dialogue #2
Mihrigul Tursun
Camp Survivor
March 2019[4]
Interview originally conducted in Uyghur

My name is Mihrigul Tursun, I am from Cherchen county. I am twenty-nine years old this year.

مەن مەھرىگۈل تۆرسۆن، چەرچەن ناھىيەسىدىن، بۇ يىل29 ياش.

I graduated from Guǎngzhōu University in 2010, and then I went to Egypt to study for my master's degree.

مەن 2010-يىلى گۇاڭجۇ ئۇنۋېرسىتېتىنى پۈتتۈرگەندىن كېيىن، مىسىرغا ماگىستېرلىق ئوقۇغىلى چىققان.

In Egypt, I met my husband, and in 2015 we had three children, triplets: two boys and a daughter.

يولدىشىم بىلەن شۇ يەردە تونۇشقان. 2015-يىلى ئىككى ئوغۇل بىر قىز، ئۈچ كىزەك پەرزەنتلىك بولدۇق.

---

4   Mihrigul and I had this dialogue not long after she arrived in the US. Throughout the conversation, you could sense the rawness of her recent traumas. Sometimes it was hard for her to organize her thoughts. Other times, her fingers were shaking as she spoke of her experiences. Often, she needed to stop to gather her composure. I told her a few times that if it was too hard we could stop any time she wanted; that it was okay if she didn't want to re-live it. But she insisted on telling her story, wanting the world to know the truth of what was happening in the camps.

It was not easy to take care of three infants, so in May 2015, I accepted my parents' help and went back home to Cherchen with my forty-five-day-old infants.

ئۈچ بالنى باقماق ئاسان ئەمەس، بلىسىز، ئۆيدىكىلەرنىڭ
«قايتىپ كېلىڭ بىز بېقىشىپ بېرىمىز» دېگەن تەلپى بولغان
باللىرىم بىلەن 2015-يىلى 5-ئايدا ۋەتەنگە قايتتىم.

After I was back in China, from that time until April 27th of 2018, I was detained three times.

شۇ ۋاقىتتىن تاكى 2018-يىلى4-ئاينىڭ 27-كۈنى مەن
خىتتايدىن ئايرىلغانغا قەدەر جەمئى ئۈچ قېتىم تۈرمىگە
سولاندىم.

* * *

The first time, I was arrested and detained for more than two months. Then they put a black bag on my head, shackled me in foot chains and handcuffs, covered my mouth, and sent me to the prison. When I arrived, they interrogated me for over three hours, asking what I had been doing outside of my homeland in the Uyghur region. The interrogations continued for three days, without letting me sleep, before I was isolated in a dark cell for seven days.

بىرىنچى قېتىم ئىككى ئايدىن كۆپرەك ۋاقىت توتۇپ تۇرغاندىن
كېيىن، ئۈغزىم چاپلانغان، بېشىمغا قارا خالتا كىيگۈزۈلگەن
قولۇمغا كويزا سېلىنغان ھالەتتە تۈرمىگە ئەكىتىلدىم. ئۈچ سائەت
ۋەتەننىڭ سىرتىدا نىمە ئىش قىلغان دەپ سوراق قىلدى. يەتتە
كۈن قاپقاراڭغۇ ئۆيگە يالغۇز سولاپ قويىدى.

After that, I was sent to the ordinary camp with others.

كېيىن باشقىلار بىلەن بىرگە نورمال لاگېرغا سولدى.

The second time I was arrested, I was put in a cell in the basement of a police station, and again I was interrogated for three sleepless days and nights. After that, I was taken to the hospital for blood testing, an eye exam, face scanning, and gynecological testing. And then they put me in a camp, cell number 210.

ئىككىنچى قېتىم تۇرمىدە ساقچىخانىنىڭ يەرئاستى ئۆيىدە ئۈچ كېچە-كۈندۈز ئۇخلاتماي سوراق قىلىندىم. ئۇنىڭدىن كېيىن دوختۇرخانىغا ئاپىرىپ قان ئېلىش، كۆز ئالمىسنى تەكشۈرۈش، يۈز شەكلىنى سكانىردىن ئۆتكۈزۈش، ئاياللار تەكشۈرۈشلىرىنى قىلىپ بولغاندىن كېيىن 210- نومۇرلۇق لاگېرغا سولىدى.

For the next three months, all my connections with the outside were cut. I couldn't get any news from my kids or my family.

شۇنىڭدىن باشلاپ ئۈچ ئايغىچە سىرىت بىلەن ئالاقەم پۈتۈنلەي ئۈزۈۋېتىلدى. بالىلىرىمنىڭ ۋە ئائىلەمدىكىلەرنىڭ ھىچقانداق خەۋىرىنى ئالالمىدىم.

*   *   *

The conditions were terrible. In the camp, there were cameras on every wall.

شارائت شۇنچىلىك ناچار، لاگېرنىڭ ھەربىر تېمىدا كامىرالار بار.

In the camp, we couldn't talk to each other. There were even some people who didn't go out for nine months from the cell. They never got to see sunshine.

لاگېردا بىز ئۆز-ئارا پاراڭلىشالمايمىز. ھەتتا 9 ئايدىن بېرى بىر ئۆيىدىن چىقىپ باقمىغان، كۈن نۇرى كۆرۈپ باقمىغان ئادەملەر بار ئىدى.

94

We couldn't shower, and we couldn't wash our hands and faces frequently.

يۇيۇنالمايتتۇق، يۈز-كۆزىمىزنىمۇدائىم يۇيالمايتتۇق.

The lights went off at 9 p.m., but normally it was impossible to sleep because the cell smelled gross (because there too many people, and none of them could shower).

كەچ سائەت 9 چىراقلار ئۆچۈرلەتتى. ئەمما لاگېرنىڭ ئىچىدىكى سېسىق پۇراقتىن ئۇخلاش مۇمكىن ئەمەس (ئادەم جىق، يۇيۇنغىلى بولمىغاندىكىن سېسىق پۇراپ كەتكەن).

Because of how crowded the cell was, we could only lie down on one side. And every two hours we switched with the people who hadn't had enough space in the first round.

ئادەم جىق، ئورۇن يېتىشمىگەچكە، ھەر ئىككى سائەتتە بىر نۆۋەت ئالمىشىپ، يانپاش، قىستىلىپ ياتاتتۇق. يەنى ھەر ئىككى سائەتتە بىر، ئالمىشىپ نۆۋەت بىلەن ئۇرە تۇراتتۇق.

If thirty people lay down at first, the other twenty waited for their turn as a group standing against the wall. And then we'd switch every two hours.

30 ئادەم ياتسا 20 ئادەم تامغا قاراپ ئۇرە تۇراتتى. ئىككى سائەتتىن كېيىن 20 ئادەم ياتسا قالغانلار ئۇرە تۇرىدۇ. ھەر ئىككى سائەتتە مۇشۇنداق نۆۋەت ئالماشتۇراتتى.

In the morning, we were required to tidy up the bedding in a strict army style.

ئەتىگەندە ئورنىمىزدىن تۇرغاندا يوتقاننى چوقۇم ئۇلچەملىك ھەربىي ئۇلچەمدە يوتقان يىغىشىمىز كېرەك ئىدى.

Even though the bedding was very dirty and thin, if we couldn't make the bed as perfect as the army standard when the examiner came, they would punish us by withholding food. They used this as an excuse to beat us up, or to deny the daily food to everyone in the camp cell.

شۇنچىلىك كىرلىشىپ كەتكەن نەپىزلا يوتقانلارنى ئەگەر ئۇنداق ئۇلچەملىك يىغالمىساق، تەكشۈرۈشتىن ئۆتمىسە تاماقتىن جازالىناتتۇق. تەكشۈرۈشتىن ئۆتەلمىسە شۇنى باھانە قىلىپ تاياق يەىمىز ياكى لاگېردىكى ھەممەمىزگە تاماق بېرىلمەيدۇ.

For breakfast, we were given "rice soup." You know how when you wash rice the water turns white? It was like that.

ئەتىگەندە «شىفەن» دەيدۇ، يەنى «شووگۇرۇچ» لېپكىن ئۇ «شووگۇرۇچ»مۇ ئەمەس. گۈرۈچنى سۇدا يۇسا ئاقۇش سۈيى چىقىدىغۇ، ئەلمان قىلىپ شۇنى قايىنتىپ بېرىدۇ.

Sometimes you might find all kinds of things were in that soup, like metal strands from a steel wool scrubber. I couldn't eat for the first three days. It was disgusting.

بەز ىدە ئىچىدىن ھەرخىل نەرسىلەرچىقىدۇ. يەپ، سىم يۇغۇچ دېگەندەك. باشتا ئۇچ كۈن ئىچىپلا كۆڭلۈم ئېلىشىپ ئىچەلمەي باشقىلارغا بەردىم.

Later, I was so starving, and I couldn't bear it. I had to live! So I had to drink that soup.

كېيىن قورسىقىم بەك ئىچىپ كەتتى. چىدىمىدىم، ياششىم كەرەكتە، ئىچمەي بولمىدى، ئىچتىم.

At noon, they gave us two steamed buns, which were as big as an egg, and hard and moldy and smelly. They threw them at us as we if we were dogs. Sometimes mice poop fell out of the buns. But in order to live we had no choice except eat to them, even though they could never really keep us full.

چۈشتە تۆخۆمچىلىك چوڭلۇقتا كۆكىرىپ سۆپىتى ئۆزگىرىپ قىتىپ كەتكەن، پۇراپ كەتكەن ئىككى تال كىچىك موما ئەتقا تاشلاپ بەرگە ندەك بىردۇ. بەزىدە ئىچىدىن چاشقانلارنىڭ مايىقى چىقدۇ. ياشاش ئۈچۈن يەيمىز، ئەلۋەتتە تويمايمىز.

*   *   *

Three months after I had been detained in the airport, I was released for the first due to my triplet's health.

مەن بىرىنجى قېتىم ئايرودرۇمدا تۇتۇلۇپ كەتكەندىن كېيىن يەنى ئۈچ ئايىدىن كېيىن، بالام تۇگكەپ كەتكەن ۋاقتتا، ئۈچ پەرزەنتىمنىڭ كېسەل سەۋەبىدىن، تۈرمىدىن كېپىللىككە قويۇپ بېرىلدىم.

When they released me, they put my ID card, passport, and telephone on a blacklist, a way to mark me as "Suspicious."

تۈرمىدىن كىملىك، پاسپورت، تېلىفۇن نومۇرۇم ھەممىسى «قارا تىزىملىك» يەنى «گۇمانلىق» دېگەن بەلگە قويۇلغان ھالەتتە چىقتىم.

The day after being released, I learned that my kids were being operated on in the children's hospital in Ürümqi. But I didn't know why or what for. Only that they did the exact same operations on the same places on all three of them, including their necks.

تۈرمىدىن چىققان كۈنۈمنىڭ ئەتىسى ئۈچ بالامنىڭ ئوپىراتسىيە قىلىنغانلىقىنى ئۇقتۇم. نىمە سەۋەپ بىلەن ئوپىراتسىيە قىلىنغانلىقىنى ئۇقمىدىم، ئۇرۇمچىدىكى بالىلار دوختۇرخانىسىدا ئۈچ بالامنىڭ ئوخشاش يىرىدىن يەنى بويىنىدىن ئوپىراتسىيە قىلىنغان ئىكەن.

They said that two of my children withstood the operations, but that one of the boys had died during the procedure. Then they placed my son's corpse into my hands.

بىر ئوغلۇم بىر قىزىمنىڭ بەرداشلىق بېرەلىگننىي بىر ئوغلۇمنىڭ بۇ ئوپىراتسىيەگە بەرداشلىق بېرەلمەي جان ئۈزگەنلىكنى ئېيتىپ، بىر ئوغلۇمنىڭ ئۆلگىنى قولۇمغا بەردى.

Now I have one daughter and one son left.

هازىر يېنىمدا بىر ئوغلۇم بىر قىزىم بار.

*   *   *

During my second interrogation, in April 2017 . . .

2-قېتىم سوراق قىلىنغان ۋاقىت 2017-يىلى 4-ئاي

. . . I am sorry, these memories makes me so and comfortable sad . . . They interrogated me for three days without letting me sleep.

...كەچۈرۈڭ، بۇ ئەسلىمىلەر مېنى بىئارام قىلىۋەتتى ...ئۈچ كېچە كۈندۈزئۇخلاتماي سوراق قىلدى.

They asked what kind of people I'd communicated with when I was outside of my homeland . . . . Sorry. . . .

ئۇ جەريانىدا ۋەتەن سىرتىدا قانداق ئادەم بىلەن ئالاقىلاشقان دېگەندەك سۆئاللارنى سوراپ... كەچۈرۈڭ...

. . . In addition to torturing me physically, they showed me many pictures of people I didn't know, asking questions about them, which, of course, I didn't have answers for.

جىسمانىي خورلاشدىن تاشقىرى، مەن تونۇمايدىغان نۇرغۇن ئادەمنىڭ رەسىملىرىنى كۆرسىتىپ سۆئاللارنى سوردى. مەن ئۇقمايدىغان سۆئاللار.

98

First of all, I have no connection with politics. Secondly, I would not be a traitor to my homeland.

بىرىنجىدىن مېنىڭ سىياسەت بىلەن ئالاقەم يوق،
ئىككىنجىدىن ۋەتەن ساتقۇنى خائىن ئەمەستىم.

"I went to Egypt as a regular student, and then I came back because I had triplets and needed my parents' help. I'm just a human being who was arrested for that." I answered their questions that way.

مەن نورمال ئوقۇش بىلەن چىققان، ئۈچ پەرزە نتىم بار
بولغانلىقتىن ۋەتەنگە قايتقان ۋە شۇنداق تۇتۇلغان بىر
ئىنسان، ئۇقمايمەن دەپ جاۋاپ بەردىم.

Because I didn't have the answers they wanted, they tortured me again, and again, and again. They beat me harshly until blood ran from my nose and mouth, and there were times when they used electric shocks.

ئۇلار خالىغان جاۋابنى بەرمىگەنلىكىم ئۈچۈن يەنە قايتا-
قايتا قىيناشلارغا ئۇچرىدىم، قاتتىق ئۇرۇپ ئېغىز-بۇرنۇمدىن
قان چىقىرىۋەتكەن، توكقا چىپتىپ قىينىغان ۋاقتىلار بولدى.

*   *   *

They shocked me. The shaved my head. They fed me drugs to interrogate me. And during this period, they tortured and abused me not only physically, but also mentally. They tore up my right eardrum with their beatings and their torture.

توكقا چىپتىلدىم، چىچىمنى چۈشۈرۈۋەتتى، دورا يىگۈزۈپ سوراق
قىلىندىم. بۇ جەرياندا جىسمانى ۋە پسىخكا جەھەتتىن
قىينىدى تۇرمىدە سوراقتا قىيناش، ئۇرۇش جەرياندا ئوڭ
قۇلىقىمنىڭ قۇلاق پەردىسى يىرتىلىپ كەتتى.

*   *   *

They were disappointed that they couldn't get useful information from me, so they made me take a white pill.

هىچقانداق ئىشلەتكۈدەك جاۋاپلارغا ئۇچۇرغا ئىگە
بولالمىدۇق دەپ ماڭا بىر ئاق رەڭلىك دورىنى يىگۈزدى.

I lost all sensation after I ate it.

مەن ئۇ دورىنى يىگەندىن كېيىن مەندە ھىچ قانداق سزىم
قالمىدى.

The thing I'm afraid most of is a fierce dog getting loose and attacking me. But after taking the pill, even that wouldn't have scared me. I didn't feel any sense of fear.

مەن ئەڭ قورقىدىغان ئىتتقا تالاتماقچى بولۇشتى، لىكىن
مەندە ھىچقانداق قورقۇش سزىمى بولمىدى.

Then I felt like I was flying in an imaginary world. After that I don't remember anything they asked or what I answered.

ئۆزەمنى خىيالى دۇنيادا ئۇچۇۋاتقاندەك ھىس قىلدىم.
كېيىن ئۇلا نىمە سۇئال سورىدى مەن نىمە دەپ جاۋاپ
بەردىم بىلمەيمەن.

*   *   *

Because they thought what I had to say was useless, the authorities began to taunt me with things like: "Your parents passed away while you've been here."

ئۇلارمۇ كار قىلمىغاندىن كېيىن، ساقچىلار ماڭا «سەن
تۈرمىدىكى چاغدا داداڭ ئۆلۈپ كەتتى، ئاپاڭمۇ ئۆلۈپ كەتتى»
دەپ مېنى روھى جەھەتتىن قىيناشقا باشلىدى.

Or: "Your second son died at the hospital yesterday, now you're left with only your daughter . . .

«تۇنۇغۇن ئوغلۇڭ دوختۇرخانىدا جان ئۈزدى، ھازىر بىرلا قىزىڭ
قالدى..

. . . now she is blind, so, we gave her to others as an adoption."

‏...ئۇنىڭ كۆزى كۆرمەسكەن، باشقىلارغا بىقىشقا بىرىۋەتتۇق»

Or: "We arrested your brother and sister too. They are on the way here now . . .

‏«سىڭلىڭ بىلەن ئاكاڭمۇ تۇتتۇق، ھازىر يولدا كېلىۋاتىدۇ...

". . . and they also will be thrown in prison and sentenced to life . . ."

‏...ئۇلارنىمۇ شۇ تۈرمىگە تاشلايمىز، مۆددەتسىز كىسىلدۇ»

". . . but you will be given the death penalty. However, before you die, you'll need to you confess everything . . .

‏...ئەمما ساڭا ئۆلۈم جازاسى بېرىلىدۇ، ئۆلۈشتىن ئاۋۋال ھەممىنى
ئىقرار قىلىشىڭ كېرەك...

" . . . and, at least, you will get some mercy. By not confessing up to now, you've already destroyed your parents' and your kids' and your relatives' lives—your whole family."

‏...ئىقرار قىلساڭ ھېچ بولمىسا كەڭچىلىك قىلىمىز، ئىقرار قىلماي
ئاتا-ئاناڭ، بالىلىرىڭ، ۋە بىرتۇغقانلىرىڭنى پۈتۈن ئائىلەڭنى
ۋەيران قىلدىڭ.»

Hearing that was harder than any of the other torturing, including the beatings, drugs, or electric shocks.

‏بۇنىڭ بىلەن ماڭا ھەر قانداق ئۇرۇش،
دورا يېگۈزۈش توكقا چىتىشلار،
قىيناشلارئىبغىر كەلمىدى.

Why? Because I really thought that what they were saying was true.

‏نېمىشقا؟ چۈنكى مەن ئۇلارنىڭ دېگەنلىرىنى راست
دەپ ئويلاپ قاپتىمەن.

During my stay in the camp cell, I witnessed the deaths of nine women.

شۇ تۈرمىدە تۇرۇش جەرايىندا مەن ياتقان لاگېردا توققۇز ئايالنىڭ ئۆلۈمىگە شاھىت بولدۇم.

* * *

During the third detainment, they interrogated me for two days and nights, but without much torturing. However, I had to wear orange jail clothes.

ئۈچىنچى قېتىم سوراق قىلغاندا مېنى ئىككى كېچە ـ كۈندۈز سوراق قىلدى، لېكىن بۇ قېتىم بەك قىينىمىدى. ماڭا ئاپېلسىن رەڭلىك كىيىم كىيگۈزدى.

Besides the orange uniforms, there also were blue ones. The blue uniforms were for detainees who were not sentenced or not charged with a specific crime and for those who were just being detained temporarily.

ئاپېلسىن رەڭلىك كىيىمدىن باشقا كۆك رەڭلىك كىيىملىكلەر بار، كۆك رەڭلىك كىيىملىكلەر تېخى تۈرمىگە كەسىلمىگەن، جىنايىتى ئېنىقلانمىغان ياكى ۋاقىتلىق تۇتۇپ تۇرۇلغانلار.

The orange clothes meant a person would be given the death penalty in China. I lost all of my hope at that time.

ئاپېلسىن رەڭلىك كىيىمنى خىتتايدا ئۆلۈمگە ھۆكۈم قىلىنغانلار كىيىيەتتى. ئاشۇ ۋاقىتتا مەن ھەممە نەرسىدىن ئۈمۈدنى ئۈزۈپ بولغان.

* * *

I was told, "It's impossible for you to take one step away from Cherchen; we will cut off your head if you try to."

ئۇلار «سىننىڭ مۇشۇ چەرچەن ناھىيەسىدىن يىراققا بىر قەدەم مېڭىپ بېقىشىڭ مۇمكىن ئەمەس، كاللىمىزنى كەسسەپ بېرىمىز سەن مۇشۇ يەردىن چىقىپ كېتەلسەڭ» دېيىشتى.

102

I never thought that I could escape what was happening in China.

مەنمۇخىتايدا يۈز بېرىۋاتقان ئىشلاردىن قېچىپ
چىقىپ كېتەلىشىمنى ھەرگىز ئويلاپ باقمىغان.

However, because my two children (and the one who had died) had entered China with Egyptian passports, China was obliged to send them back to Egypt, and because of this, I was able to be saved.

ھايات قالغان ئىككى بالام ۋە ئۆلۈپ كەتكەن بالام مىسىر
پاسپورتى بىلەن خىتايغا كىرگەن بولغاچقا ئۇلارنى مىسىرغا
قايتۇرىۋېتىشمىز دىگەن سەۋەپ بىلەن، ئىككى دۆلەتنىڭ
ئارىلىشىشى بىلەن قۇتۇلۇپ قالدىم.

The Chinese government gave me a two-month limit to bring my children to Egypt, and then, after that, I would have to come back to China.

خىتاي ھۆكۈمىتى بالامنى ئىككى ئايغىچە مىسىرغا ئاپىرىۋېتىپ
كېلىشكە رۇخسەت قىلدى. ئە مما چوقۇم خىتايغا قايتىپ
كېلىشىمگە بۇيرۇق قىلدى.

They threatened me by saying that if I didn't return, then they would kill my parents, my brother, and my sister who were in the concentration camp.

ئەگەر قايتىپ كەلمىسەم مېنىڭ ئاپام، دادام، ئاكام ۋە سىڭلىم
ھەممىسى تۈرمىدە ھەممىسىنى ئۆلتۈرىۋېتىدىغانلىقنى
ئېيتىپ تەھدىت سالدى.

They said, "If you love them, and you want to see them alive, you'll have to come back and never tell people what had happened to you and the others who were with you in the camp."

ئۇلار «سەن ئۇلارنى ياخشى كۆرسەڭ، ھايات كۆرىدىسەڭ
چوقۇم قايتىپ كېلىشىڭ كېرەك .يەنە تۈرمىدە كۆرگەن، ساڭا
ۋە سەن بىلەن تۈرمىدە بىللە ياتقانلارغا نېمە ئىش
بولغانلىقنى ھېچكىمگە ئېيتماسلىقتڭ كېرەك.

"You'll have to keep it secret. If you want your relatives alive, you must come back to China after you take your children to Egypt."

«بۇ يەردە يۇر بەرگەن ئىشلارنى سىر تۇتۇشۇڭ كېرەك. ئاتا-
ئاناڭنى، ئۇرۇق تۇغقانلىرىڭنى ھايات قالسۇن دېسەڭ، ئىككى
بالاڭنى مىسىرغا ئاپىرىپ قويۇپ قايتىپ كېلىشىڭ كېرەك»
دېدى.

I gave them my promise. Before they released my from the camp, they dressed me in beautiful clothes, put make up on me, and had me tape a video.

مەن ئۇلارغا ۋەدە بەردىم. تۈرمىدىن قويۇۋېتىشتىن بۇرۇن
ماڭا چىرايلىق كىيىملەرنى كىيگۈزۈپ، گىرىملارنى
قىلدۇرۇپ، مېنى سىنغا ئېلىۋالدى.

On the video, they made me vow that the Chinese government never hit me or insulted me. I said I would return to China after I brought my children back to Egypt. I said I loved China.

سىن كۆرۈنۈشىدە، ئۇلار «خىتاي مېنى ئۇرمىدى، تىللىمىدى،
خورلىمىدى. مەن بالىلىرىمنى مىسىرغا ئاپىرۋېتىپ جۇڭگوغا
قايتىپ كېلىمەن، مەن جۇڭگونى سۆيىمەن» دېگەندەك
قەسەملەرنى بەرگۈزدى.

*   *   *

I couldn't find my husband after I got to Egypt because he'd been arrested. I hadn't known about it because I'd lost all of my connections while I was detained.

مىسىرغا قايتىپ ئېرىمنى يولدىشىمنى تاپالمىدىم، چۈنكى
مېنىڭ ھەممە ئالاقەم ئۇزۇلگەندىنكېيىن، يولدىشىمنى تۇتۇپ
ئېلىپ كەتكەنىكەن.

It turns out, he had gone to China look for me, but he got arrested at the airport. I don't know if he is alive or not.[5]

يولدىشىم مېنى ئىزدەپ ماڭغاندا ئايرىدرۇمدا توتۇپ كېتىپتۇ. ھازىرغا قەدەر ئۇ ھاياتمۇ ئەمەسمۇ بىلمەيمەن.

Where could my children go? If I had to leave them in Egypt while I went back to China, I would one hundred percent die from grief.

ئەمما بالىلىرىمنى ئاپىرىپ قويىسام كىمگە تاشلاپ قويىمەن؟ تاشلاپ قويۇپ كەتسەم مەن يۈزدەيۈز ئۆلىمەن.

If I'd given up my life to return to China in order to save my family, then the world wouldn't know what happened in my homeland. No one would know the girls and women who died. It will remain a secret forever.

ئەمما ئۆزەمنى ئۆلۈمگە تۇتۇپ بېرىپ، ئۆيىدىكلەرنى قۇتقۇزۇش ئۈچۈن بارسام ۋەتەندە بولۇۋاتقان ئىشلار، ئۆلۈپ كەتكەن قىزلار، ئاياللار ھەممىسى سىرلىتى قالىدۇ، دۇنيائۇقمايدۇ.

*   *   *

Jewher: How long have you been in the US?

سىز ھازىر ئامېرىكىغا كەلگىلى قانچىلىك بولدى؟

Mihrigul: It will be five months on the 22nd of this month.

ھازىر مۇشۇ ئاينىڭ 22 سى كەلسە 5 ئاي بولدۇ.

Jewher: Where did you go first after being released from prison (camp)?

تۈرمىدىن چىقىپ ئاۋال قە يەرگە باردىگىز؟

---

5   In a recent conversation, she told me finally was able to communicate with him, and that he is back in Egypt.

Mihrigul: First I went to Cairo. Then the US Congress brought me to America.

تۆرمىدىن چىقىپ ئاۋال مىسىرغا باردىم، قاھىرەگە،
كېيىن ئامېرىكا كونگرىسى ئامېرىكاغا ئەكەلدى.

Jewher: Was there anybody who was waiting for you?

سىزنى بۇ يەردە كۈتۈپ تۇرغان ئادەم بارمىتى؟

Mihrigul: No. There was no one.

ياق، ھىچكىم.

Jewher: You came directly?

ئۇدۇۇلال ئامېرىكىغا كەلدىڭىز؟

Mihrigul: The US government saved me. They immediately brought me here.

شۇ ئامېرىكا ھۆكىمىتى جىددى ھالەتتە قۇتقۇزۇپ ئەكەلدى.

*   *   *

They disappeared Uyghur culture. With that, one day they will disappear the Uyghur people. I can't face up to my parents and brothers and sisters and relatives.

ئۇيغۇر مەدەنىيىتىنى يوقتىتۇۋەتتى. شۇنىڭ بىلەن
ئۇيغۇرلارنىمۇقىرىپ تۈگىتىدۇ. مەن ئاپام، دادام
ئاكام، سىڭلىم ۋە تۇققانلىرىمغا يۈز كېلەلمەيمەن.

I hope they understand my choice and will forgive me.

ئۇلارنىڭ مىنى كەچۈرىشىنى، توغرا چۈشىنىشنى ئۈمىد
قىلىمەن.

Because I think that only by revealing the experiences of what happened to me and others in the camps in these ways, can I face the souls of those women who were killed in front of my eyes.

چۈنكى مەن مۇشۇنداق سۆزلىسەم شۇ كۆز ئالدىمدا ئۆلۈپ كەتكەن شۇ ئاياللارنىڭ روھىغا يۈز كەلەلەيمەن، دەپ ئويلايمەن.

I'm not only speaking for myself, I am trying to speak up and be the voice of the people in the camps.

ئۆزۈم ئۈچۈن سۆزلىمەيمەن، ئاشۇ لاگېردىكىلەرنىڭ ئاۋازى بولۇپ تۇرۇپ سۆزلەۋاتىمەن.

PART 5

Changing the Uyghur Region

Population Data Collection Form
人口信息采集表

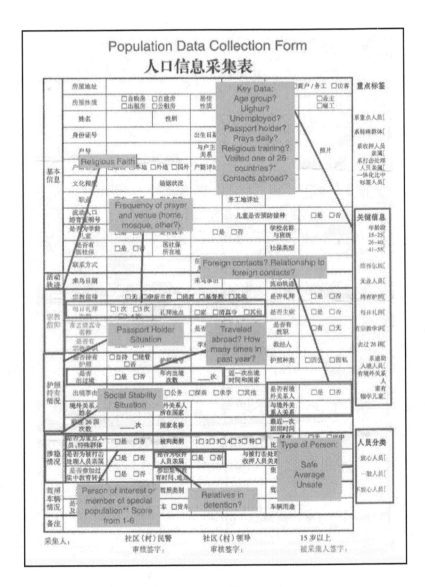

Population Data Collection Form

The Camps

There are all kinds of reasons you can be sent to a camp. It could be because you have a Twitter account or a VPN that allows you to search overseas information or contact people there.

And there is the issue of the degree to which you practice your religion. I spoke with a person who told me that one morning at 2 or 3 a.m., there were ten to twenty people sneaking out of their building to dump their prayer mats in the sewer drains. It was, of course, humiliating. But they understood what it would mean for them to be caught having prayer rugs in their homes.

Authorities in the Uyghur region circulate a "population form" to collect people's information. They ask your name, your gender, your ethnicity, and your ID number. Do you pray? How many times a day do you pray? Do you own a passport? Have you been traveling abroad? Do you have relatives who have been detained and/or arrested? Do you have family members who have passports? Do you have family members who have traveled abroad? It's basically a points system. The higher you score, the more trouble you may face. Having a passport can equal a point. If you have "prayed five times a day," it can count as more points.

However, it is important to say that it's not as though everyone ends up in the same kind of camp as Mihrigul Tursun. There are different types of them.

Indeed, there may be some camps that are educational. You learn Chinese. You learn how to sew things, how to make shoes, how to put sheets on—just as you might see in the so-called "proof of life" videos that the authorities make to promote the idea that the camps are for poverty alleviation purposes and are beneficial to Uyghurs. These are the camps that often are used as propaganda for tourists and journalists.

From there, you'd likely be sent to pure labor camps. You just work and work and work, lucky to get paid eighty cents per hour. As the Coalition to End Forced Labour in the Uyghur Region has explained so clearly:

"The Chinese government is also transporting Uyghurs and other Turkic and Muslim-majority peoples to other parts of China, where they are working in factories under conditions that strongly indicate forced labor. Reports in 2020 revealed that the forced labor of Uyghurs and other Turkic and Muslim-majority peoples has been expanded beyond the Uyghur Region, with at least 80,000 Uyghurs or other Turkic and Muslim-majority peoples transferred to factories across China where they cannot leave, are under constant surveillance, and must undergo "ideological training" to abandon their religion and culture. Recent video evidence shows that some of these transfers occurred in early 2020, when much of China was under lockdown as a result of the expanding COVID-19 outbreak. This means these laborers were forced to work and exposed to the virus while much of the country's population sheltered at home."[6]

In addition, firsthand accounts tell us that there are other kinds of camps where you get beaten and tortured. Some people go to the beat-and-torture camp first. There, the authorities try to investigate you, to interrogate you. If finally they find that there's "nothing wrong with you," you get transferred to the camps that

---

6 Coalition to End Forced Labour in the Uyghur Region, "Call to action on human rights abuses in the Uyghur Region in the apparel and textiles sector," updated October 2020. Visit: enduyghurforcedlabour.org/call-to-action/

are not treating people as "harshly"—essentially, the "training and vocational" centers.

Because so many people are arrested, released, and re-arrested multiple times, as of now it is difficult to know the exact number of people locked up. It's very fluid. And it is very massive. Based on the increased number of centers (and their sizes), as well on the food waste and the energy production, experts estimate there are 1 to 1.8 million people who have been arrested and detained in those camps. And according to the Chinese government's own white paper published in September 2020, a yearly average of 1.29 million people went through "vocational training" between 2014-2019. If these numbers were even accurate, that would mean that at least 10% of the Uyghur population in the region had been in one of the so-called vocational centers.

It is so painful to watch not only what is happening to individuals but also what is happening to my culture and my history—the way in which, through very careful calculations, it is being systematically erased.

Sinicizing the Uyghur Region

In some Chinese government documents and interviews of Chinese government officials, it says that Uyghurs' minds are "heavily polluted with extremist ideology;" the government only is helping to educate them by taking the poison out of their brains. That is the official stance. It also claims that Uyghurs are not educated and that they are low-income people. The authorities say that they are helping Uyghurs by giving them job opportunities. But, okay, let's give them the benefit of the doubt, let's say their goal really is to create job opportunities and lift people up. What about the doctors being "re-educated"? The professors? Singers, soccer players, rappers? That argument just doesn't hold. Anyone who has contributed to the Uyghur society in a positive way has been arrested.

What does hold is that it is clear that they want to destroy all of the Uyghur culture and its community in the region and turn it into an extension of Han China.

The percentage of Han Chinese living in the Uyghur region has increased dramatically. In the 1953 government census, the Uyghur region was 75% Uyghur and 6% Han Chinese. (The balance was made up of the other 11 ethnic groups in the region). As of November 2020, the number of Uyghurs has been reduced to the 44% range, while the Han Chinese population has increased to 42%. Most importantly, because the Uyghur region is 1/6 of China's mass land and vastly underpopulated, for the Chinese authorities, the effrorts for migration have also helped them to solve the overcrowding issues in the traditional Han regions.

And they are succeeding, it seems. Slowly and carefully, Beijing is working to eliminate our culture in every small way.

Even the street names have been changed. In 2018, officals began renaming many things that had overtones of religiousness and/or were specfic to Uyghur culture. So now what used to be in the Uyghur language has been changed to very Chinese names. Meshrep Road became Healthy Road. Another traditionally named road was changed to Bright Road. And on and on. It's absurd.

Sometimes it is not always so small and subtle. An investigative piece in *The Guardian* showed wide-scale destruction of mosques in the Uyghur region. To understand the scale of this, the article states that "Out of 91 sites analysed, 31 mosques and two major shrines, including the Imam Asim complex and another site, suffered significant structural damage between 2016 and 2018."

But worst of all: the sterilization. I knew it was happening from Mihrigul Tursun's testimony when she said that the women were given certain medicines, and afterward no one was menstruating. That meant they could not get pregnant. In the beginning, I suspect the authorities were experimenting, trying the drugs on those women to see if they would work. But soon, it clearly fit into their larger plan.

Now, there are reports that Han Chinese men are being sent to sleep in the same bed with Uyghur women. The official line: it's supposed to create more bonds between the Han Chinese families and the Uyghur families. Imagine how difficult this was when most of the men were in the camps. In one instance, many, many Uyghur girls were married to Han Chinese men at the same time, in a single ceremony; the girls in some villages were told that if they got married to Han Chinese men, they'd be granted eighty thousand yuan, and they would get a car, or their children would go to school for free, or they would be guaranteed housing. Again, the authorities won't admit it is about diluting and eliminating Uyghur culture. Instead they say it's strengthening the bonds between the Han Chinese and the Uyghur people.

So then why, when you see the images of the mass wedding, are those girls crying? Presumably because they know if they don't do it, they or their parents will be sent to camps. Even worse for some, they may be accused of inciting ethnic separatism. The Chinese government fully understands what it is doing.

If you are one of those girls, here are your options: Will you choose to get raped in the camps and have your parents die in there? Or do you want to marry and get money?

Who wouldn't choose the second one?

During the Qing Dynasty, the Shunzhi Emperor was paranoid about having his regime threatened. If anyone wrote anything that could even possibly be taken as criticism, he would burn all their books. Any speeches or thoughts that threatened the regime would lead to someone being arrested. It was called the "literary inquisition," also known as "speech crime." And I honestly see that happening right now in the Uyghur region. I imagine the government probably will continue to allow some Uyghur dance and music and restaurants—those all attract tourists, which is a big part of the Uyghur region's economy. But there is no doubt that the language and the writings are going to be strongly affected. For the past few years, many universities shut down their Uyghur Literature Studies programs, while many others replaced educational textbooks aimed at teaching about Uyghur culture.

Can Uyghur culture be revived?

For now, I don't see that happening. I suspect the attacks on us will only get worse and worse. I think that the authorities in Beijing are working to sacrifice this generation, with the hope that the younger generation will become completely Sinicized. If that happens, they believe there won't be Uyghur-Han Chinese problems anymore, and no one will ever threaten the Chinese regime again.

I truly believe this is what they, in the spirit of Shunzhi, are working for.

Finding Uyghur Pride

Six years ago, with my limited Uyghur language, I would not have been able to interview those camp survivors. I would not have been able to understand what they said. When Mihrigul appeared before Congress, her testimony was translated. The words she chose in Uyghur perfectly reflected what she was feeling inside, an experience that English just couldn't fully capture. Listening to her words in English, you would never feel the same. Learning Uyghur brought me closer to other Uyghurs, and it also strengthened my commitment to fight for our culture.

I don't know if it was intentional, but I started cooking more Uyghur food at about the same time I started learning the language at IU in Bloomington. In the past, I'd cooked Chinese food to save time. I could make a meal in fifteen or twenty minutes. Uyghur food is more complicated and takes a lot longer. However, because it is made in bigger pots, you can eat it for several meals. And having those Uyghur meals set me on a mission that also made me "more Uyghur." I wanted to share Uyghur food with all the Chinese people in Bloomington. Why I wanted that is difficult to explain. It wasn't revenge or anything like that. It was more of a response to the idea that the government wanted to assimilate us to Han Chinese.

Okay, well I'm going to assimilate your stomach to Uyghur.

I wanted to try spreading my culture somehow. I danced Uyghur dances in any possible event when I was at IU. I wanted to let people know who Uyghurs are.

I attended every possible lecture that talked about Uyghurs. I wanted to be there to say that I was Uyghur. That way, people wouldn't feel that Uyghurs were so far away from them. *Here is one right in front of you.* I wanted to show my identity to others.

Even when I lived in Beijing, when I heard about bad things happening to the Uyghurs, I wanted to defend them—even surrounded by Han Chinese. There is a very specific negative tone that we all recognize when some Chinese people identify us as Uyghurs. In Beijing, I could clearly hear it when I might be telling someone that although I was raised in Beijing, much of my family lived in the Uyghur region. "It's the same," they would answer. "It's all Xinjiang people," said with a tone that really was saying, *You are all same: cockroaches.*

I heard that tone here from a Canadian who had gone to mainland China and heard things about Uyghurs. It was at IU, and we'd been talking, and he said: "Oh, I didn't know you were Uyghur."

I bristled inside. It was spoken in that tone I hadn't heard for so long, but one that was instantly familiar. Anyone who has been discriminated against because of their identity is familiar with this tone. When you experience it face-to-face and hear people talking like that, it is something that becomes a part of you.

When my dad was teaching in the university as an economics professor, he told me that so many people would say, "You teach in a university? That's so rare for Uyghurs." It was all part of the stereotype that Uyghurs are not smart. They're not hardworking. They're poor people. They're thieves. He said, "We should never have to hear such comment. One day I don't want a Uyghur being a professor to be a surprise." My dad really wanted to help with the development of the Uyghur region and the perception of Uyghur people.

The more someone wants to take the thing that belongs to you, the more you cherish it. And that's what is happening to me. It's happening to lots of Uyghurs, actually. And it's made me understand what my dad was thinking.

Before he got arrested, I blamed him. *You made this happen. You made me stay so far away from our family and left me alone here in the US.* After he got arrested, that turned to: *Oh, why did they do this to him? He didn't do anything that was bad enough to deserve to be arrested like this.* And then after he was sentenced, that evolved to: *How could they do this to my father?* The more I understand about his work and his vision, the more I understand why he took so many risks on behalf of Uyghurs. It makes me look up to him more.

Here is the bottom line: As with so many other Uyghurs, I'm still just a daughter who is trying to help out her family. It's just that my family has been increasing and expanding. Uyghur people are my family.

I'm not a politician. I studied political science in school so I could understand the language of politicians—from those in the Chinese government to those who can help us in the US, the European Parliament, and other parts of the world. I needed to learn their language to help my people. But I don't consider political language to be my language.

I am just a daughter. A Uyghur daughter.

PART SIX

A Period of Awards,
Recognitions,
and Nonstop Work

October 2016
Martin Ennals Award

Yaxue Cao, the cofounder of China Change, had been really invested in my dad's case—both by fighting a lot on his behalf and by promoting his ideas, even publishing a collection of his work. In 2016 it was Yaxue who brought up the idea of the Sakharov Prize. She suggested to Elliot that they should lobby for it in Europe for my father on my behalf. Elliot didn't know her very well at that time, and of course, he was more than a little protective of me. He told Yaxue it sounded okay but, "I'm going to Europe with you."

Together they went. The two of them mostly were trying to inform members of the European Parliament about my father and educate them about the Uyghurs. Remember, at that point, nobody knew much about who we Uyghurs were. Now, for example, when I talk about the Uyghur people, I can start with saying, "Do you know there are over one million Uyghur people in the concentration camps?" But back then, you had to start with the basics: "Uyghurs are a Turkic Muslim majority peoples living in . . ."

At the same time the Sakharov was being pursued, there was a push for my father to be nominated for the Martin Ennals Award for Human Rights Defenders, another important human rights award in Europe. My dad had already received an award from PEN American Center in 2014, and now it seemed he might be on the verge of getting even more international attention.

Though we were hoping any action we undertook could change everything, honestly Elliot and I didn't expect any of those awards to get him out of jail. But we knew it could change how he was treated in prison. Because according to Hu Jia, the previous Chinese Sakharov Prize winner, his own condition in prison had greatly improved after he was honored. So that's what we were hoping could happen for my father too.

When the call came in about the Martin Ennals Award, I was meeting with someone from the European Parliament in a coffeeshop in Geneva.

I was in Europe for twelve days, the allotted time for my visa. I'd come to Geneva during the period when the Ennals announcement would be made. I wanted to be ready. Normally people get a visa for up to three months, but I only got twelve days. They didn't want me to stay for even one more day, suspecting that I might be a refugee who planned to stay there and never go back. I remember so many people were investing their time trying to help me be able to leave the country *and* come back safely—from Scott Busby at the State Department to my lawyer Wade Thomson. Elliot bugged them all the time. Finally, after several months' effort, I'd gotten the Schengen visa the day before I was supposed to travel to Europe.

On the call in the coffeeshop, I learned that the Martin Ennals jury had made its decision. "Please do not tell anybody yet," my contact said, "but your dad got the award. Don't tell it to anyone else because the other finalists don't know yet."

I was really happy. This was one of the major human rights awards in Europe. And I thought: imagine what a bonus it would be if my dad also were to be a finalist (or even winner!) of the Sakharov Prize from the European Union. And then, strangely, within the hour I received another phone call from Lucia Parrucci, a woman I knew at the Unrepresented Nations and Peoples Organization (UNPO), who had helped to push for the Sakharov Prize. She wanted to let me know that my dad would not be getting the award this year. Apparently, there were concerns about upsetting China, especially since the activist Hu Jia had already gotten the Sakharov Prize in 2008. She said it seemed very unlikely that the committee would give another Chinese citizen this award for some time.

While I was pretty disappointed at that news, I was still so happy about the Martin Ennals.

Elliot was mad about the Sakharov news. He was *really* mad. He thought everyone should support my dad—one hundred percent, without any hesitation. In the same way that Elliot's passion could make him very emotional, it was in Yaxue's personality to remain rational in the face of setbacks. After analyzing the situation and the landscape, she'd begun to prepare me for the fact that it did not look good for a Sakharov nomination. And once we got the final word, while Elliot was fuming, Yaxue was being more positive. She told me, "Even though he didn't get the award, I think we already won. Everybody in Brussels now knows who Ilham Tohti is, and they know who Uyghurs are. That's the first huge step. Part of the victory."

Yaxue was right. Before she and Elliot went to Europe to lobby on behalf of my father, not many of those politicians knew about the Uyghurs or my dad. Only people in academia seemed to know about my father. Yaxue told me we would work on the Sakharov Prize for another year.

I don't think Elliot was refusing to accept the reality; he just was always mad when people didn't show support for my father. "Why don't they give it to Ilham Tohti? He's the best. He should get most of the awards!" Elliot would probably have stayed mad for forever if my dad had not eventually won it. I know Elliot. He was just such a sweet person, and he always was so supportive of my father and me.

February 2019
The National Prayer Breakfast

I was invited to the National Prayer Breakfast. There, I was assigned to sit with the Prince and Princess of Serbia. At the table next to me was the Vice President of Taiwan. I was really surprised. I just thought it was going to be a breakfast.

President Trump was there too.

Two tables over were the Secretary of State and the Ambassador of Religious Freedom.

I kept thinking: *Why am I here? Why am I arranged to sit here?*

I glanced over when I saw Nancy Pelosi waving at me. I looked all around. I couldn't believe she'd be waving at me. How could she possibly remember me out of the hundreds of people she meets every day?

It still feels kind of magical, unbelievable to me. I don't know how I've come to where I am today. But on the other hand, I did spend over five years working really hard to reach this point, even if I don't always know how I got here. Only God knows how much I have been through. Sometimes I still don't understand. I just wish my father were here. Life is so weird.

July 2019
The Oval Office

Two days before I went to the White House, I'd been invited by the State Department to be a keynote speaker at the Ministerial to Advance Religious Freedom. Later that day, I was on the Hill to attend another event when the phone rang. "I'm so sorry," I said. "I'm really busy now. I'm just about to go to deliver a speech."

"We're calling from the White House. We just wanted to ask you if you'd consider coming here to meet with the president. . . . If you were given this opportunity, could you tell us what you would say if you only had fifty seconds."

My speech was coming up in nearly three minutes. I had to get on stage. But at the same time, if I wanted the opportunity to meet with the president to advocate for Uyghurs and my father, I had to come up with something that was fifty seconds long *and* would meet their satisfaction.

I just started talking, and before long they cut me off, saying "Okay, okay. Thank you."

From the tone of their voice, I thought they were not satisfied. I was pretty certain I'd doomed it, ruined my chances.

They explained that I was one of a few candidates who were recommended, and that they would get back to me by the following morning. If only I'd had more time to prepare.

I never heard back from them. Okay, fine. At least I didn't even think about having to say something at the White House.

Two days later, I was back at the Ministerial conference at the State Department. Ambassador Sam Brownback came up to me and said, "I'm taking you to the White House in a few hours."

"What? . . . Okay!"

He said, "It's only going to be a media event with other human rights survivors. Nobody will have a chance to speak. It will be a photo session."

The next thing I knew we were boarding a fancy bus with Ambassador Brownback. Like a tour guide, he was standing in the middle of the bus holding two seats, explaining to us what the protocol would be and everything else.

At the White House, we had to lock up our phones and our bags. One Tibetan lady had a traditional white scarf hung over her shoulder that she wanted to give to the president. But even that was not allowed. Watching how it all worked was interesting. Around us were several soldiers or army officers in white uniforms, all handsome and tall, standing and waiting for President Trump to come.

In the Oval Office, they kept emphasizing, "Ms. Ilham, please stand next to Ambassador Brownback." I didn't really know why, other than that maybe they just wanted me to be in the picture more.

It all was taking a lot longer than I expected. For just a picture?

And then President Trump came in. With the media still waiting outside, the president thanked us all for coming. He said, "I know it's been a long day for all of you." And then he started showing us some of the furniture, telling us about the paintings he'd brought in, the chair he'd switched out, and other aspects of the Oval Office.

I was a little confused, thinking: *Why is he acting this way*? He seemed very different than how he appeared on TV, where he often looked mean and arrogant and sometimes rude. Instead, he was being very gracious.

Lots of things were flooding through my mind. From: *Is that really his hair?* to: *Why is it so hot in this room?* to: *I just want to get it over with and go home; I'm exhausted after being up since 6 a.m.*

Then they let in the press, and everything changed. Suddenly, he acted different. He got stiff. Serious. He pulled out his speech and started reading with a tight facial expression. For the second time I thought: *Why is he acting this way?* Five minutes ago, he was so relaxed and gracious, and then he got so edgy once the media was present.

Out of nowhere, a Tibetan survivor among us said, "Oh, Mr. President!" As she started to say her piece, the staff tried to stop her. Remember, this was only supposed to be a photo session in the Oval Office. President Trump interceded. "It's okay," he said. "Let her say it."

After she spoke, the staff changed their position and said we all could speak briefly. But it had to be short "because the president is very busy. He needs to catch a helicopter."

All I could think was that I needed to have my chance because otherwise, once the time ran out, he would leave. My mind went into overdrive, trying to think about what I was going to say.

Why hadn't I memorized something to say, just in case?

I sensed one of the staff members was about to end the meeting. You could tell from her body language. But before she could say anything, I jumped in. "Mr. President, there are one to three million . . ." I said it very loud so everybody could hear what I was saying.

He turned his head to me.

I barely remember what I said at that point; I was so eager to get his attention, so he wouldn't leave.

I continued: "There are one to three million Uyghurs locked up in concentrations camps, including my father, who is locked up in a prison."

He interrupted to ask, "Oh, where is it in China?"

"West part of China. In English, we call it the 'Uyghur region.' In Chinese, it's called 'Xinjiang.'" I wasn't sure which name he knew the name for the region, so I wanted to say both to make sure he knew what I was talking about, even though I knew saying "Xinjiang" might upset some Uyghurs.

He stopped me before I was finished. "How long?"

"He's been locked up for six years. The last time I heard of him was 2017."

"Oh, that's tough stuff."

And then, just like that, he was gone, off to the helicopter.

I felt like I was dreaming. And I kept trying to go over what I'd said. Did I say it well? Did I make too many grammatical mistakes? Did I get the important message out?

Looking back, and having watched it on various videos, I can see how nervous I was and how much pressure I felt. I was trying to squeeze all the important information—my dad, the camps, what is happening with the Uyghurs, who the Uyghurs are—into fifty seconds or less. And on top of that, because he kept interrupting with questions and comments, I had to keep reorganizing my thoughts. To be frank, I was a little disappointed because it didn't seem like he knew much about the situation of the Uyghurs. But even still, it was an important moment for my advocacy work and for me, and it helped lead to me being invited to participate in September's United Nations General Assembly forum.

September 2019
United Nations General Assembly

The night before the UNGA event in New York, I was coughing my lungs out. And once I finally fell asleep, it didn't last long. My roommate was also sick, and her coughing kept me up all night. I had to wake up at 6 a.m. in order to be at the UNGA event for a 9 a.m. event. Things had to be ready. I still had a fever that morning. And my throat was burning.

Before I spoke, there were still three possible versions of my speech: the White House's, the State Department's, and my own. I was concerned about having to use the one that started, "Hi, my name is Jewher. I'm a Chinese Uyghur. I'm from the West part of China, Xinjiang Uyghur Autonomous Region." My concern was that in Chinese the word "xīnjiāng" means "new territory," a term that reminds many Uyghurs of the history of being occupied and colonized by China. In recent years, Uyghur people in the diaspora have become more and more sensitive about the terms used to describe our homeland, due to the persecution of the last few years. Eventually I was able to work it out and bring some flexibility to the language of the speech.

I hope that, despite having a fever and feeling so dizzy, I spoke strongly on the Uyghur people's behalf among so many powerful figures, including, on my panel, the president, the vice-president, the secretary of state, and the UN secretary-general.

October 2019
Sakharov Prize

In 2019, the nomination letter for the Sakharov Prize was renewed. One of my dearest friends, Lucia Parrucci of UNPO, played a huge part. She emailed every single MEP for their support. I remember one of her colleagues telling me, "You really need to thank Lucia and her co-worker Sophia." This colleague said you could see dark circles around their eyes because they'd been typing all night. And there were others in Europe who also contributed quite a bit to advocating for my dad's nomination. I was truly grateful they were there and willing to put in so much effort, as it would have been too difficult for Yaxue or me to travel to Europe every time we wanted to talk with someone.

I was hopeful this time around. You could see the attention increasing year by year. Day by day. People now knew more about what was going in China. The camps were in the news. And people couldn't hide from it anymore. No one could ignore it and say, "Oh, I didn't know about that." Everybody at the governmental level understood what was happening.

And for me, even though I still was fighting for my dad, I also was very aware that this no longer was just about him anymore. It was about the entire Uyghur community.

On the night of the announcement, as usual, I couldn't sleep. I was looking at my phone and watching for Lucia's texts from the Parliament. She was able to watch the debate surrounding the three finalists, which then would be followed by a vote. After that, the winner would be announced.

Lucia texted that the Greens were being very supportive of my dad. But then The Left in the European Parliament (GUE/NGL) was opposing it, worried about their relationship with China. One of the MEPs, Mr. Bütikofer, later told me that some of his colleagues received a letter from the Chinese officials trying to talk them out of voting for my father for the award. Some of the letters reportedly had threatening overtones.

It's intense, she texted. Then she said we had 63 votes. There was a huge chance he might win this time.

I had one thought running through my mind: "Oh my God. Oh my God. Oh my God. Oh my God. Oh my God."

And then Lucia followed-up with the great news.

But they wouldn't announce it until the next day. So I couldn't tell anyone.

Here's the thing: I can't keep a secret from my roommate and best friend, Yusra. I tell her everything. I can't even hide a surprise in front of her. "Yusra," I yelled. "I can't tell you, but oh my God!" And then after five minutes: "Okay, I'm just going to tell you. He won! He won!"

Later Lucia video-called me, and we were both crying, tearing up and saying how happy Elliot would've been to hear this.

I think we cried out of missing Elliot more than the joy because we really, really wanted him to see it.

Of course, at the award ceremony there were Chinese officials from the Embassy. It was funny because our crew, who was filming it for a documentary, was sitting right behind them.

Lucia also was seated just behind them. She later said that there were three points in my speech when everybody stood up and applauded. The Chinese officials were the only ones sitting down. Lucia told me that I should've seen the looks on their faces.

Later, I ran into some Chinese people at the hotel. They'd caught my attention because I could tell they were Chinese. And they could tell I noticed. And there, for a moment, we were just staring at each other.

The very first time I did my public testimony for Congress in 2014, I was so nervous about Chinese officials being present. I remember asking if they would be there and being told, "It's a public hearing. Anybody can come. In fact, they will come. They come to every hearing." I almost had a panic attack when I heard that.

Now I don't mind. I'd even welcome the chance to meet with them and engage in conversation.

But it's not like I'm fearless. I am still afraid of the government. Afraid that they are going to harm me, my family, or any other Uyghur people. But since the news of the camps became public, I now imagine being able to have a calm face-to-face conversation. I would tell them, "I'm not recording this conversation. It's only you and me. Nobody else. Now, can you tell me what you really think? I really want to understand. Because what is happening in the camps is not something I'm fully capable of understanding. Can you explain?" I'd ask if they really believe in something that the majority of people find so inhumane, or if they are just supporting it because this is their job.

Over the past seven years, not one Chinese official has ever directly reached out to me. So many Uyghurs I know have been intimidated by the government. But I've never been contacted directly. It's something that kind of surprises me.

If the Chinese group outside of the hotel had been government officials, I think I really might have asked them those questions. I just wanted to understand what they really thought.

A Common Question

The most common question I was asked at all these events: "Is there any news about your father?"

Each time, I had to say, "I wish I knew. I really I wish I knew." Then I'd pause before saying the final truth. "I don't know anything about my father anymore."

Dialogue #3
Akida Paluti, Daughter
Mother: Rahile Dawut
         (Disappeared December 2017)
December 2020

Jewher Ilham: Can you tell me when and why you came to the United States?

Akida Pulati: I came in 2015 for graduate school at the University of Washington, studying Information Systems. It had been my plan to study abroad when I was at the University of International Business and Economics in Beijing, where I'd majored in e-commerce as an undergraduate. Originally, I'd planned to major in accounting, thinking I'd want to become an accounting professor. But because of the college entrance examination system in China, the accounting program only accepted one or two Uyghur students at that time. I was not one of them. In China's education system, they accept the student first, and then your major is based on your scores. So while I was one of the top ten Uyghur students to get into the University of International Business and Economics, another Uyghur girl who had chosen accounting at the same time had had higher scores than I did. There were only so many spots for Uyghurs.

Jewher Ilham: I didn't grow up in the system. Because I was from Beijing, they didn't apply that Uyghur policy to me. It's different if you're from the Uyghur region. There, it depends on your birth certificate.

Akida Pulati: Our admissions are different than the Han Chinese's admission. After we finish examinations and apply for the university we want, we're given handbooks about the many universities in the country, and the book tells us how many ethnic minorities each school is accepting. This university is taking one hundred. That one twenty. My university accepted ten ethnic minorities who sat for exams in the Xinjiang region. So really we are competing with ourselves.

Jewher Ilham: In the United States you have so many more options. You know, the American Dream, and everything else that goes with it. To be honest, the competition is way less than in China, where everybody's dying to get in. Basically, in China, if you fail to go to college, people think you are over. And for Uyghurs or other ethnic minorities like Tibetans, sometimes even having good grades doesn't mean you can get a good job. Even having connections is not a guarantee of anything. All because of our ethnic identity. A lot of jobs say, "No Uyghurs, no Uyghurs," or, "No Tibetans." They have requirements like that. I remember one of my dad's articles talked about how Uyghurs need equal job opportunities. My cousin graduated from Beijing Institute of Technology (北京理工大學), one of the top schools in China. Even though she was a top student, she failed to get the job because she was Uyghur. The interviewer even told her straight out, "Don't you know why we can't hire you? Because you are Uyghur. You are from Xinjiang." But if you have overseas experiences and education, I think that can make up for it a little bit.

Akida Pulati: That is what I hoped for. And even though my mother insisted that I eventually come back to Ürümqi, my hope was that studying in US would give me a better chance at getting a good job.

Jewher Ilham: So you didn't plan to stay here?

Akida Pulati: I figured I'd be in America long enough to study in a top school, improve my English, and get expertise in my field. Then I'd go work in a big firm or company back in Beijing or Shanghai (or Ürümqi if my mother had her way), maybe get promoted, and have this kind of simple life. That was my plan.

At that point, it never would have occurred to me that I'd have to stay here because of the concentration camps and the need to speak up about them. I never would have imagined my mother would be disappeared. My only thoughts were about what my life would be like after I graduated. I never would have pictured that I'd become an activist, speaking out on behalf my missing mother.

*   *   *

Jewher Ilham: Your mother was also at the University of Washington as a visiting scholar, yes?

Akida Pulati: In 2016. She stayed here for six months, leaving around October or September. I often think about being at the airport when she was getting ready to leave for her flight. My mother just looked at me and said, "You are going to be back home next year." In the meantime, she said I should use all this time in the United States to gain some experience. Once she was back in China, we'd talk right after she woke up in the morning (her time). She always looked so sleepy in the video call. But after five minutes, she'd become fresh, and we would talk until I had to leave to do my evening things, and she went to the university for her work.

Jewher Ilham: Was this over Skype or WeChat?

Akida Pulati: WeChat.

Jewher Ilham: And how often?

Akida Pulati: On average, we would have a thirty-minute conversation every day or two. Of course, there were some times when I was just too busy, and I'd just leave a voice message.

Jewher Ilham: I also used to talk to my dad every day. But not on WeChat—I didn't want him to see my posts. In fact, I even secretly blocked him. What a terrible daughter! Instead, we used Skype to chat almost three times a day. It was especially important during my first few months in the US. I didn't know anybody. I needed someone to talk to. I needed to be close to my family. But the more friends I made, the more impatient I got about spending time chatting with my dad. I would find excuses to talk less with him. And now I regret it a lot. But I am glad that during those months we were able to talk so often. I'd trade just about anything to have that chance again.

Akida Pulati: I know just what you are saying.

Jewher Ilham: When did you find out your mother was disappeared? How did you find out? Did someone tell you?

Akida Pulati: It was just a typical day. I'd left her a voice message about a conversation I'd had with a professor; pretty much what I often did, reporting all the things happening in my life. In the past, I could expect that she would leave me five or six voice messages each day, exchanging ideas, making suggestions. But on that day, she left a voice message that said, "I'm going to go to Beijing today, and I will call you back after I arrive there." I didn't think much of it. This sounded normal to me because my mother traveled all the time for her research. When I was in high school, she was always packing her stuff, saying that I'm going to go to Turan or Beijing or this place or that place. I was used to it. On this day, I responded to her message: "Good luck! Safe trip!" But she didn't reply. Usually when she arrived in another place, she would call me. I tried calling. No answer. I started thinking the worst—like maybe the aircraft crashed. All kinds of bad things. I called my dad. My grandmother. They looked so calm. Peaceful. Nothing that said there was anything terrible happening at the house. "Be patient," they told me. "Your mother probably is busy doing some serious work."

After a couple of days passed with no information, I kept interrogating my dad. "Just tell me what happened," I said. "Be honest." He answered that I had to believe him, that my mother was "doing some serious work, and she might come home tomorrow." When I look back on it, I wonder if some government official had been telling my family that "Rahile Dawut is just gone for several days, but she will come back home."

At the time, I was so naïve about what was happening to Uyghurs. I only used Facebook to look at dog pictures or cat videos. I never read any news about Uyghurs. I didn't use Twitter at that time. I only went online to use the internet or social media to watch funny stuff. But by coincidence, around the time my mom disappeared, I started seeing news about Uyghur detention centers. Stories about the camps started popping up in my social media; friends began sharing news from Google. I couldn't believe what was happening.

"Tomorrow" turned into one month. And still no information about my mom. At that time, I already knew about the disappearances of the scholars. I already heard about the Yalqun Rozi, Tashpolat Tiyip, all those people who had disappeared. All I could think about was: "Has this also happened to my mom? Is she in one of these re-education camps?" And the more I read, and the more I asked around, the more I started to believe it was true.

Jewher Ilham: And once you confirmed it, what was your reaction?

Akida Pulati: At first, when I knew my mother was detained, I was devastated. I could barely function for that first month in January. And I'd had so many things I'd been planning to do. Apply for a job. Apply to the University of Washington's PhD program, whose deadline was right around the corner. But after that news, I couldn't function. I didn't write my personal statement. I didn't do anything. All I could think was, *What is happening to this world?*

Jewher Ilham: And when did you decide to do something about it?

Akida Pulati: After one or two months, I began to recover from the shock. I even had a little bit of hope. I'd heard rumors that people were being released after three to six months. Maybe, I thought, I have to be patient and wait for these next several months to pass. Not say anything about it. At that time, as an international student from China, I had a lot of concern about doing anything that would be seen as political, especially when it came to issues about Uyghurs. I didn't know what to do. Should I speak out, or should I stay silent? If I were to speak out, would it affect my other family members? I was just so confused for a while, until, at a certain point, I began to lose any hope that China would release my mother. And because the loss of my mother was very devastating for my family as a whole, I decided I had no choice but to speak out.

Jewher Ilham: And when was that?

Akida Pulati: 2019.

Jewher Ilham: I also had a period of time when, after my dad got arrested, I didn't know what to do. And I was waiting, and I didn't know how long I should wait. My family also was concerned about me speaking up and getting involved in politics. I probably would have taken longer if it wasn't for Elliot. In fact, if it wasn't for him, I probably would have gone back to China right after my dad's detention. Cluelessly flown back. I probably would've thought, *Beijing's still a safe haven for me. Even though something happened to my dad, nobody will touch me.* I was too naïve. Thank goodness for Elliot.

Akida Pulati: I also thought about going back to China when my mother first was detained. I had no one to talk to anymore. And I needed to talk to a person. Otherwise I would go crazy. That's why I considered going home. I was very serious, even when people around me started saying that I shouldn't think that way. No one could talk me out of it. But then a strange coincidence happened. One night before I went to sleep, I'd been trying to apply for job in Beijing. While on the web, I randomly came across an article about Uyghur students who'd studied abroad going back home and being detained. It got my thinking even more confused. Somehow I saw it in a positive way. Maybe the camp would not be so bad. Maybe I could stay in the camp for one month, and they would release me after they saw that I was innocent. That's how I was thinking. How lonely I was. I was *really* considering it. How naïve! But then I came across another article about how bad these camps and prisons really were—beatings, physical and psychological torture, and long sentences. That was when I realized the idea of going back to China at this time was crazy. I am so thankful I came across those articles. Every time I'm about to make a stupid decision, it seems like God is there to protect me.

Jewher Ilham: In 2019, who were the people who helped you figure out what you could do and how you should do it?

Akida Pulati: To be honest, when my mother first was detained, I kind of kept to myself, maintaining a distance from the world. I wasn't in touch with many people. Mostly I just tried to do my work while having all those crazy thoughts about going back. Some people were saying, "Why don't you speak up for your mother?" But as I said earlier, I was avoiding politics, afraid the Chinese government would punish my family or me if I spoke out. My family's safety was and is my first priority.

Still, I kept asking myself, "Should I speak out? Should I speak out?" I asked the advice of some very wise people. "Should I speak out? What's your opinion? What are the best *and* worst scenarios?" They would go through everything, but no matter what, they always ended by saying that the choice to speak out or not was a decision I needed to make—they couldn't make it for me. So, I listened. Evaluated. And then one day, I finally looked in the mirror, and I decided: *I will speak. I will speak out.*

After I made that decision, I moved on to asking people, "*How should I speak out?*"

I contacted the photographer Lisa Ross in New York (also a friend of my mother's), and we reached out to *The New York Times* opinion page. This is how things started. Lisa Ross has been an important person to me.

Jewher Ilham: We all had someone there.

Akida Pulati: That's true.

Jewher Ilham: I think it's quite crucial, you know? With these kinds of circumstances, we need the mental support.

Akida Pulati: No one ever taught us about what to do when faced with all the things that happened in our lives over these past several years. It's very hard to make a wise decision on our own. We need to consult with other people.

Jewher Ilham: To be honest, I still don't always know if I made the right decision. I have no clue. But I do know that advocacy work was my only chance at making my dad's circumstances better. But what I don't know is if it worked or if it might have made things worse. That's something I'm still trying to figure out.

Akida Pulati: I'm trying to figure that out too. Also, I think about it because it's not just my mother being detained. There also are relatives, some close and some distant. They don't have anyone to speak up for them. And as much as I've wanted to speak up for them, it's hard for me to get information about their situations.

Jewher Ilham: There have been some people who've gotten released. Maybe we have triggered a change.

Akida Pulati: You never know . . .

*　　　*　　　*

Jewher Ilham: Akida, do you know why your mother was targeted? Do you think it was just for being Uyghur or a Uyghur academic, or was there something in her work that was particularly threatening? Did she have a history of being in conflict with the party authorities?

Akida Pulati: To be honest, I was so confused at first. Was the Chinese government targeting intellectuals and writers just like they'd targeted the good people a thousand years ago? Was this really like in the Qing Dynasty or Ming Dynasty? I was getting that kind of feeling. My mother never publicly spoke up about anything. Quietly, she just did her research, her teachings. Just read her books. Her research was all about the customs of traditional life in the Uyghur village, their celebrations, their funeral rituals, their Meshrep, their songs. And all her research would get approved by the Chinese government before it went public. She knew in advance if there was something wrong with her research. She even delivered speeches about her research at Beijing Mínzú University, and other institutions. When I was a college student in Beijing, I went to see my mother speak. If there was something wrong with her research, she wouldn't have had the chance to give a speech—the system in China never would have allowed it. Not to mention that she's such a cautious person. I once asked my mother on WeChat if she'd heard that people's passwords were being confiscated. Her answer: "Don't talk." She never wanted to get into any trouble.

When she came to the United States, she made several foreign friends, even Han Chinese friends. She cooked meals with them, just leading a simple life. No contact with any political people. Never. No contact with other Uyghurs. She's just such a simple person. So law abiding.

I guess I am still confused. It's very hard to figure out what kind of actions or statements will trigger the Chinese authorities. But in this crazy system in China, even the most law-abiding person can somehow trigger an angry response from the Chinese government.

It's hard for me to think about that.

Jewher Ilham: Now I'm just guessing, tossing ideas out there, but supposedly there's a population data form that was released in the Uyghur region, and it asks for information such as how often you pray, whether you are a passport holder, which countries have you visited overseas, whether you have family contacts outside, et cetera. If you meet several of the criteria, then you are considered a "suspicious person." So first of all, with our parents, they are Uyghur: that's the most "suspicious" part, and that's their "biggest crime." And along with all those other questions, having an education also becomes a top concern. According to the government's thinking, educated people are dangerous because they know how to use their words as their weapons.

They're basically trying to erase our culture and erase our language. But maybe they focused on your mom because what she does as an academic is to do introduce people to the Uyghur culture. It's the opposite of what government wants. Maybe that's one of the reasons.

Akida Pulati: This is what I am thinking exactly—especially after what I've witnessed happening to our homeland. And, yes, I also heard about those forms around the time when my mother first disappeared. Did you know that along with my mother, several intellectuals in my family circle also disappeared? For example, my uncle, a founder of a software company in Ürümqi. I read in the news about his disappearance. And another distant, very intellectual uncle is also being detained. Each time I read or hear something like this, I just keep asking myself if the Chinese government is crazy. They just want ruin the lives of the smartest people.

Jewher Ilham: I wonder when does this end.

Akida Pulati: I don't know.

Jewher Ilham: I do believe it will end. It's just a matter of time. But I just wonder when.

*   *   *

Jewher Ilham: How is your life now? Are you finding a path that you want to be on?

Akida Pulati: It's complicated. Much like what you were saying earlier, I'm not 100% sure if my speaking out will make my mother's situation better or worse, but I feel like I need to do it. It wasn't that long ago when the work in my field required me to focus every day for eight to nine hours. Business. Budgets. All of those things. Get up at six or seven o'clock, go to work, and then come home at the end of the day so tired, have a shower, have a sleep, and then the day ends. It was just like that. But everything became really hard to balance once politics entered my life.

At least I feel like I am doing the right thing. Nothing I'm going to regret. We will figure out our life in the future.

Jewher Ilham: How about your friendships? Do you think your advocacy interfered or changed those aspects of your life? In my case, maybe I was supposed to go shopping with my friends, watch movies, just have fun. But I didn't even feel like it. Because I had to attend this meeting or that one to speak up about my father and the Uyghur people.

Akida Pulati: You are describing the same things that I am experiencing. Exactly. Several years ago, I would just hang out with friends and talk about things like clothes or makeup for several hours. Right now, I don't have time. How can I when there are more serious things to consider? So yes, while my social life has been reduced to a large extent, one of the good things is that I've made friends during my political activity. Like you! I'm talking to you now! It's not like I don't have friends because I am activist. It's more that my friend circle is a little bit changed.

Jewher Ilham: One thing I am grateful for, with these advocacy experiences, is the people I've met. I really am grateful for what I have. But I do want more. I can't be completely satisfied because I still wish to be able to communicate with my family and have my father freed, my cousin freed, everyone freed. I do want those things too. But for where I am now in my life, I am grateful for what I have.

Akida Pulati: Yes, during this whole awful process, we encounter very genuine people who want to help unconditionally. And sometimes, because we are just so focused on the work we do on behalf of our parents and people, we cannot always see who is unconditionally supporting us. But I know they are there. We all know. Because of them, we are managing our lives so much better.

PART SEVEN

Rest and Inspiration

A Needed Break

Just before the pandemic caused the shutdown, I was traveling so much to the point of being overwhelmed. And looking ahead at my calendar, I knew the advocacy work was only going to get busier by mid-March when I was scheduled to begin forty days of events in Europe.

Looking at my datebook, I thought to myself: *I need a break.*

I convinced my roommate Yusra to come with me to Europe for two weeks before my work was set to begin, to celebrate her birthday. We were just going to relax and to have fun.

In January we began planning, booking flights to Paris and Milan. It felt like such a luxury, the thought of just being a tourist.

By late February, I was already aware of the coronavirus. I'd been buying masks, at that time more concerned about the Chinese tourists in the US who may not have known if they were infected. I urged my friends to get masks, telling them that they needed to be ready and prepared in case something worse happened. But still, that was only February. The virus still felt like more of a worry than something that would end up being so devastating.

On March 5, the day before we were supposed to travel, Milan was shut down and along with it our flights. Shortly after, all of the March advocacy events were cancelled: Luxembourg, Spain, Switzerland, the Netherlands, France, Italy, and one at the European Parliament in Brussels.

And then masks started going out of stock.

That was the moment when I understood the true depth of the pandemic.

Nothing

When everything was canceled, I was mad about it. But at the same time, it was a huge relief. Having an empty calendar made me realize how much I needed to rest. I could breathe a little. From that time in mid-March, like everyone else, I began quarantining. And I didn't feel like doing anything. Not watching TV shows. Not even cooking. The most I'd do was to soak in the bath for hours, listening to music, and then I'd just melt into my bed.

Ahhh. It felt nice to do nothing. It felt really good.

Seeking Motivation

From March to May, my brain was blank. I was barely sleeping. A lot of the time, I'd just lay in bed and stare at the ceiling, spacing out and not really thinking about anything. I was just enjoying taking slow breaths and going into myself.

Ever since I'd come to the United States when I was eighteen years old, I worked nonstop. I'd had to be the responsible one of my father's three children, taking care of everyone. Plus, taking care of myself. Taking care of finishing my education and keeping an income. And, of course, taking care of the advocacy.

This quiet was so nice! No plans or commitments. No thoughts about responsibilities. It felt good not to think about anything.

I felt kind of greedy. Almost a little addicted to it. This pace of life started to feel a little *too* nice.

Every day I'd tell myself it was temporary. *Just a little more time*, I'd think. *I just want to rest a little bit longer.*

I ignored emails. Didn't accept phone calls.

To be honest, I'd lost some motivation.

I was afloat. Stepping on a cloud one minute and then feeling like I might be tripping and falling off it. As the months went on, one moment I could be very comfortable and then the next so empty.

It seemed like every other day I swung from being contented to feeling really guilty. Like a battle between my selves, with one telling me, "You should be motivated; you've got responsibilities," and the other saying, "You deserve this. You have worked so hard. You need this rest."

Growing plants and vegetables was the one small thing that made me start feeling more energetic. I'd wanted to grow as much as I could to not have to go out for groceries.

I just looked on YouTube: *What are the easiest vegetables to grow?* First I saw scallions, which I used every single day when I cooked. And I loved celery, so I grew that too. I cut off the top part of a bok choy I already had, and I put it in water, and it started to grow. It was so beautiful. So amazing.

Taking care of them daily—watering them, moving them into the sunlight—created a routine to my life, one that I'd lost. And I started thinking: *Maybe I need to grow. Maybe I need to be strong again.*

I began realizing that maybe this way of life had gone long enough. It finally started to feel really wrong. I knew I needed to stop being the way I was. I needed to put myself together. But it was like I was stuck in quicksand.

If it hadn't been for Yusra, my best friend and roommate, it might've lasted beyond May. She really helped me and encouraged me by saying, "I think you should really pull yourself together."

"I'm gaining so much weight," I told her. "I'm not taking care of myself. Everything is going downhill. I should not be giving myself up like this. Or losing my energy and motivation."

"It's okay," she said. "It's understandable. You've done a lot. I know you were tired."

"But I can't make this pandemic my excuse anymore. This way of life has been going on too, too long for me." And then I made Yusra promise that every time she saw me not wanting to do anything, she would scold me. Tell me I needed to get back to work.

Yusra nodded and agreed. "You've had enough rest," she said. "It's time you get going."

As I said earlier, I feel lucky because someone always appears in my life at the right moment to help me achieve something. Sometimes I think they don't even recognize how much they've meant.

And if I told them, they'd probably shrug their shoulders and say, "I didn't do anything." But I hope they know how those little, tiny gestures—a little, tiny push or even one single sentence—literally have made me a different person, a better person.

Picking up Again

But it's not like I immediately started back into the advocacy. It was more like a slow rebuilding. Growing plants. Exercising. Baking bread, cakes, and sweet desserts. Even beginning to watch TV shows again. Slowly adding things into my daily life instead of doing nothing. From there I began reading lots of articles, listening to podcasts, and then talking with friends.

All that made me regain some motivation again, regain an interest in life.

Slowly, slowly. Day by day.

Sometimes you can get so worn out by your work, your life, and even those things that you are most passionate about. I'm here to say that it is normal. It is okay. Everyone needs time to reflect and to reconnect with what inspires them.

Part of what re-inspired me was the Black Lives Matter movement, particularly all that was taking place during the pandemic. With that, I remembered how important awareness is, and it also made me think about how I wished Uyghurs had this same level of attention too. If you disappear for a little bit, then the attention of the world moves on to another subject quickly. It's almost like if you stop posting about the Uyghur issue, people might think it's no longer an issue. They'll assume that if the main advocates are not talking about it, then the Uyghurs probably are doing just fine. Watching those protests, I was inspired by them. And in terms of advocacy, it made me realize what a big mistake it had been for me to disappear for two-to-three months.

Once I got going, I found myself completely engaged again. It feels as if it runs in my blood. I found I could just pick right back up immediately. And not only did I continue my own work for my father and the Uyghur people, but thanks to encouragement from Sophie Richardson, I also began working as a Program Associate for the Worker Rights Consortium (WRC), which is an independent labor rights monitoring nonprofit organization. My job—now as a Forced Labor Project Coordinator—is to focus on the forced labor issues in the Uyghur region and address the supply chain of products coming out of there.

WRC's main objective, as stated on its website is "to document and combat sweatshop conditions; identify and expose the practices of global brands and retailers that perpetuate labor rights abuses; and protect the rights of workers who make apparel and other products." As one of the leading and founding members of the Coalition to End Uyghur Forced Labour, WRC allowed me to connect with so many global NGOs, advocates, experts, and ethical businesses, in order to join forces to combat the egregious human rights issues affecting my people.

It was inspiring to be around so many smart people again, who not only were so kind and caring, but were so much passionate about their work. (And it was bonus to see that my supervisor Penelope looked like one of my favorite actors, Anne Hathaway!) I got to be involved in researching brands who were directly and indirectly profiting from Uyghur forced labor. And among other things, I have learned many effective tools for change, such as the Coalition's Call to Action, which asks brands and retailers to:

Stop sourcing cotton and other raw materials, yarn, textiles, and finished products from the Uyghur Region. Since cotton and yarn from the region is used to make textiles and finished goods across China and in numerous other countries, this requires brands to explicitly direct all factories that supply them with textiles and finished goods not to use cotton, yarn or other materials from the Uyghur region.

Cut ties with companies implicated in forced labour—those that have operations in the Uyghur region and have accepted government subsidies and/or government-supplied labour at these operations.

Prohibit any supplier factories located outside of the Uyghur Region from using Uyghurs and other Turkic or Muslim-majority peoples supplied through the Chinese government's forced labour transfer scheme.[7]

It's been such a blessing to wake up each morning to a job that I not only love so much, but one in which I learn new ideas and skills and ways of thinking each day.

Even though the general public awareness of the camps began around 2017, it really wasn't until 2019 that we saw a huge rise in Uyghur rights activism. With the United Nations General Assembly and the US and EU governments all addressing the humanitarian issues resulting from the camp system, the attention has brought courage to many more Uyghurs outside of China, allowing them to speak out and share their stories.

Until that point, a lot of them had been afraid. *What if we speak up, and nobody cares, and then we cause more harm to our family? What if we don't gain anything, and our efforts don't help raise awareness or get our families released?*

Of course, the reporting in the news also helped. And definitely the testimonies from the camp survivors. What was revealed triggered a lot of rage in the Uyghur community abroad. They understood not only how easy it would be for some of their family members to disappear, but they also saw what their friends

---

7 From the website for the Coalition to End Uyghur Forces Labour (https://enduyghurforcedlabour.org/faq/)

and families and community members were going through *at that very moment* in the camps—from political indoctrination to beatings to sexual abuses to forced labor and so many other unimaginable inhumanities.

It became impossible for them to ignore what was happening once they heard those testimonies. It created rage that turned into action. Every one of us knew that there was a good chance that this was happening to our own family in China.

So, yes, the Uyghurs are getting a lot of attention on the world stage. I don't know if I should be happy about it or sad about it.

Elliot's Lasting Influence

I think if Elliot were at the Trump meeting, he probably would have leaned over and whispered, "You speak better English than he does." He always tried to comfort me with some dark humor or jokes that were really not that funny. I keep a picture of him in my room, and I always look at it, imagining what he might be saying. Hoping that he is proud of me for not being so much of a "delicate jasmine flower" anymore. What would have been his facial expression if he'd been able to hear about the Sakharov Prize?

People always say, "Your father must be so proud of you," but unlike with Elliot, I don't worry anymore if my dad is proud of me or not. I just want him to be free. I don't even have to see him, as long as he can be freed and be healthy. Whether my dad is mad at me, proud of me, happy for me—it doesn't matter anymore. I just want him to be safe.

My father taught me a lot about how to be a good person by showing me how a good person acts. But Elliot took efforts to teach me how to fight for every good person to continue being a good and *free* person. He taught me how to take concrete actions. He took me up the steps, one by one.

My father, on the other hand, taught me by letting me see him do his work. His way of teaching (from which I learned so much) was: "This is how I do it. And now you can do it too."

BECAUSE I HAVE TO

Whether I chose it or not, this is my life now, and I have no other option but to continue my work. Because I have to.

Afterword

Clare Robinson, Advocacy Director
Scholars at Risk

Jewher's moving book is at once a story unique to herself and her father, and one that reflects a global campaign by authoritarian regimes to silence those who question the status quo.

Introducing us to her father, Jewher shares how Ilham Tohti used to point his finger to underscore a point. That, on that day in September 2014, he told his family he was relieved by the sentence of life in prison—"not too bad"—as it wasn't the death penalty. That he sees both the good and the bad in a thing, a person. That he would not compromise his values. That he taught his daughter how to be an activist by taking action himself. With each detail, Jewher helps us get to know her father, as we collectively try to tell Professor Tohti's truth for him, until the day he can do so again himself.

At Scholars at Risk, where I direct our global advocacy efforts, we've been working in support of Ilham Tohti, an economics professor, since July 2009. The media had reported him missing, and I remember, weeks later, the satisfaction of hearing of his August release, hoping there was something positive to come next. *Hoping* is a natural response, one that is automatic, even when we know it's not usually positive political developments that lead to releases, but rather significant, consistent, reputation-damaging pressure, combined with economic or political incentives, aimed at states engaged in oppression. In 2009, the international pressure was significant enough to result in Professor Tohti's release.

In the years that followed, Professor Tohti was watched, placed under house arrest, watched again, and harassed. Police threatened to kill his wife and children. Authorities interrogated him about his academic work. They prevented him from traveling with Jewher to take up a visiting scholar position at Indiana University in the United States. And, as Jewher shares in the opening pages of this book, they arrested him and sentenced him to life in prison. In doing so, they aimed to silence other scholars and public intellectuals who dare explore or express new ideas. The authorities saw him as an example.

> At the trial and in the prison, he was shackled—not only his hands, but there were also heavy chains on his feet. He never killed anybody or harmed anyone. Why would he need to be shackled like that?
>
> He's a scholar. He doesn't even work-out or lift weights. The only thing he ever uses is his pen, that's the heaviest exercise equipment he has.

Attacks on scholars and the broader higher education community occur with alarming frequency. Authorities and non-state actors use wrongful imprisonments and prosecutions, killings, violence, travel bans, and wrongful dismissals in an attempt to censor and silence presumed detractors. Scholars at Risk's annual report on global attacks on the higher education sector, *Free to Think 2020*, analyzed 341 reported attacks in 58 countries and territories that occurred over the one-year reporting period.

At a rate of nearly one a day, these attacks harm individuals, like Ilham Tohti, who are directly targeted, as well as their colleagues and families. Lives are lost, people are displaced, careers are given up. These attacks also undermine entire higher education systems by impairing the quality of teaching, research, and discourse on campus.

While Ilham Tohti's situation is uniquely concerning, it is also representative of a larger phenomenon of attacks on those who study, write, teach, research, and ask questions—within China and globally. In Afghanistan, we have been witnessing an entire higher education sector under threat. In Iran, scholars like Dr. Ahmadreza Djalali and Niloufar Bayani are arrested for their academic and scientific work. In Egypt, graduate student researchers like Patrick George Zaki and Ahmad Samir Santawy are in detention as apparent retaliation for their research and studies. In Belarus, Colombia, Hong Kong, Myanmar, Thailand, and beyond, students are threatened and attacked for leading movements that seek social change. Each one of these individuals is the reason why Scholars at Risk advocates for academic freedom and the protection of higher education communities worldwide.

In the book, Jewher speaks with Akida Pulati, whose mother, Rahile Dawut, a scholar of ethnography and Uyghur culture, disappeared in December 2017 and only shortly before this writing has been reported to be in prison in China. In September 2018, it was reported that Chinese authorities had issued a two-year suspended death sentence to Halmurat Ghopur, a scholar of medicine and a former president of Xinjiang Medical University Hospital, who is being held at an unknown location. In recent years, and especially since Ilham Tohti's sentencing in 2014, the numbers of Uyghur individuals disappeared, imprisoned, or held in camps has continued to climb, reaching crisis levels.

These scholars, and many more, need our support. We must seek policy changes to increase protections for scholars and students. We must consistently remind the global community of the problem of attacks on higher education. And we must seek public, governmental condemnation of these attacks.

Given the horrifyingly large numbers, it would not be possible to tell the story of each Uyghur imprisoned in China, or of each scholar attacked worldwide. So we must rise to the challenge: To tell their collective stories by telling the specific ones we know. To remind the world that governmental policies impact people, families, and communities. To inspire action for all through one moving story. Jewher does this, and through her vulnerability and persistence, reminds us, and inspires us, to continue doing the same.

August 2021

Sources & Resources

Sources

While much of the information is sourced from my own experiences, meetings with many experts, and from media accounts, I also want to direct the reader to some sources that are specific to issues I discuss in Part Five about the many cultural and systematic changes taking place in the Uyghur Region.

On the Chinese government's white paper:
  "Employment and Labor Rights in Xinjiang" (September 17th, 2020). The State Council of People's Republic of China (http://english.www.gov.cn/archive/whitepaper/202009/17/content_WS5f62cef6c6d0f7257693c192.html)

On reported brainwashing in the region:
  "'Wash Brains, Cleanse Hearts': Evidence from Chinese Government Documents about the Nature and Extent of Xinjiang's Extrajudicial Internment Campaign" (November 15th, 2019). Adrien Zenz (https://www.jpolrisk.com/wash-brains-cleanse-hearts/)

On the reduction of the Uyghur population in the Uyghur Region
  "Main Data of the Seventh National Census of Xinjiang Uyghur Autonomous Region" (June 14th, 2021). Xinjiang Uyghur Autonomous Region Statistics Bureau (http://www.xj.xinhuanet.com/2021-06/14/c_1127561201.htm)

On changing traditional names in the Uyghur Region:
"Changing place names to 'better reflect Chinese culture' in Ningxia, and 'wonderful' Xinjiang" (September 27th, 2018). Jeremy Goldkorn (*https://supchina.com/2018/09/27/changing-place-names-to-better-reflect-chinese-culture-in-ningxia-and-wonderful-xinjiang/*)

On destruction of mosques
"Revealed: new evidence of China's mission to raze the mosques of Xinjiang" (May 6th, 2019). Lily Kuo (*https://www.google.com/amp/s/amp.theguardian.com/world/2019/may/07/revealed-new-evidence-of-chinas-mission-to-raze-the-mosques-of-xinjiang*)

On reports of Han men sent to sleep with Uyghur women
"China is reportedly sending men to sleep in the same beds as Uighur Muslim women while their husbands are in prison camps" (Nov 4th, 2019). Alexandra Ma (*https://www.google.com/amp/s/www.businessinsider.com/china-uighur-monitor-home-shared-bed-report-2019-11%3famp*)

On reports of the mass wedding
"China coerces Uyghur women into unwanted marriages" (September 24, 2019). Leigh Hartman (*https://share.america.gov/china-coerces-uyghur-women-into-unwanted-marriages*)

Image of the wedding (https://read01.com/zh-sg/KDyxOR7.html#.YewWcC-B3rB)

Resources

The following is a partial list of organizations, their research, and their work on Human Rights issues affecting the Uyghur Region. Of course, there are many other organizations and individuals (too many to list) also doing important and valuable work, and for that I am so grateful.

Amnesty International
(https://www.amnesty.org/en/location/asia-and-the-pacific/east-asia/china/report-china/)

Australian Uyghur Policy Institute – Report *Uyghurs for Sale* (https://www.aspi.org.au/report/uyghurs-sale)

Coalition to End Forced Labour in the Uyghur Region (https://enduyghurforcedlabour.org)

Congressional-Executive Committee on China (https://www.cecc.gov)

Freedom House
(https://freedomhouse.org/country/china)

Human Rights Watch
(https://www.hrw.org/asia/china-and-tibet#)

PEN American Center
(https://pen.org/advocacy-campaign/freedom-of-expression-in-china/)

Scholars at Risk – Annual *Free to Think* Reports
(https://www.scholarsatrisk.org/free-to-think-reports/)

Sheffield Hallam University – Reports *Laundering Cotton* and *In Broad Daylight*
(https://www.shu.ac.uk/helena-kennedy-centre-international-justice/research-and-projects/all-projects)

Uyghur Human Rights Project
(https://uhrp.org)

Worker Rights Consortium
(https://www.workersrights.org/issues/forced-labor/)

Xinjiang Victims Database
(https://shahit.biz/eng/)